PILLS AND POTIONS

A Pharmacist's Life

ROD HUNT-SHARP

Published in Australia by Sid Harta Books & Print Pty Ltd,
ABN: 34632585293
23 Stirling Crescent, Glen Waverley, Victoria 3150 Australia
Telephone: +61 3 9560 9920, Facsimile: +61 3 9545 1742
E-mail: author@sidharta.com.au

First published in Australia 2024
This edition published 2024
Copyright © Rod Hunt-Sharp 2024
Cover design, typesetting: WorkingType (www.workingtype.com.au)

The right of Rod Hunt-Sharp to be identified as the
Author of the Work has been asserted in accordance with the
Copyright, Designs and Patents Act 1988.

All rights reserved. No part of this publication may be reproduced, stored in a retrieval system, or transmitted, in any form or by any means without the prior written permission of the publisher, nor be otherwise circulated in any form of binding or cover other than that in which it is published and without a similar condition being imposed on the subsequent purchaser.

ISBN: 978-1-922958-76-1

About the Author

THE YOUNG ROD HUNT-SHARP had an unsettled and challenging start to life. He continually had to make new friends from different backgrounds as his police officer father was transferred to stations throughout Queensland.

He secured a good scholarship examination pass at Taringa State School and then went to Brisbane Boys' College where he received full colours for tennis before matriculating to the University of Queensland. Enrolled in the relatively new faculty of pharmacy, he passed all three years to be awarded a Bachelor of Pharmacy.

Only when called up for national service did medical examinations reveal he had contracted renal tuberculosis, which was later confirmed after additional testing when he was working and travelling in the United Kingdom.

Fortunately his relatives in London included the chairman of the Port of London Authority, Viscount Simon and his wife, who provided him with accommodation at PLA headquarters overlooking the Tower of London and invited him to functions such as the River Thames Pageant.

Hospitalisation and employment at major London hospitals helped him become highly skilled in paediatric dispensing. Later, as deputy chief pharmacist at Poole General Hospital, he was for a time in charge of sterile dispensing, which was further good experience.

Eventually returning to Australia, with English wife Gillian, Rod established the Campus Pharmacy at the University of Queensland and overcame numerous professional and personal setbacks and challenges.

Rod has maintained a keen interest in tennis ever since playing competitive tennis in Under-11 years tournaments at the Milton Tennis Centre in Brisbane. As a qualified high-level professional coach, he coached GPS girls at St Peter's Lutheran College, and on his own court at Fig Tree Pocket in Brisbane.

Marriage to Gillian was a memorable fairytale wedding, with Viscount and Lady Simon standing in for his parents. 'Ten-pound poms' were in vogue when the newlyweds boarded the Fairsky and sailed home to Brisbane for a new chapter in a rich and varied life.

Rod retired after selling Campus Pharmacy in 2005. He and Gillian now enjoy family time with their children, Sara and Peter, and four grandchildren.

Rod still enjoys a gin and tonic, which he first had on the

Queen's Barge as the guest of the then harbourmaster as it led the River Thames Pageant in London and where Rod suffered his first bout of motion sickness.

To my wife Gillian, my daughter Sara, son Peter, daughter-in-law Stephanie and grandchildren Jackson, Oscar, Cooper and Zoe 4 March 2024

Contents

Dedication	vii
Preface	1
Early Childhood	5
Caboolture	8
Rosedale	12
Edmonton	19
Cairns	22
Christmas at Caboolture	37
Corruption, Tennis and Music	47
Shorncliffe and Beyond	52
The Sporting Life	86
On to University	89
The Call to Arms	98
Married Life	157

Playing Games	190
Deeks' Winning Potion	194
Steep Learning Curve	200
Sporting Education	207
More On Education	210
Investing and Accountants	213
Family Matters	223
Retirement Years	234
Travel Diary	237
Food And Drink	239
G&T and other delights	242
Conclusion	245
Epilogue	248

PREFACE

There comes a time of reflection, when one wonders about the direction of society. Since writing my short dissertation, *Operation Manipulate*, in 2009, about the role of China in the world, much has happened.

The same predictions of uncertainty have traversed the world in which we live. Many have died, others been maimed, many have been born.

Previously I wrote about climate change, which has developed into one of the great dilemmas facing us. I do not know what has prompted me to use the keyboard again as my last experience of writing resulted in rejection.

We still enjoy the best form of democracy, the Westminster system of parliamentary governance, which is the envy of those countries that seek to divide, using any tool at their disposal.

Throughout the world much has happened with the advent of yet another plague.

The years preceding 2023 were of epic proportions, thanks to a laboratory in Wuhan province in China. Much disinformation and misinformation followed. In major cities, such as New York, tandem trailers, normally used for frozen beef, became mortuaries. People were divided.

An earlier turning point for humanity was the exposure of the horrors of war in the press releases from the war in Vietnam. Today, the tabloids are even more vigorous in their current affairs reporting. There is no better evidence than in the reporting on the Covid pandemic. Clearly there should be an enquiry, or royal commission into how it was handled in Australia.

The ill-preparedness and overreaction, lockdowns and masks, to mention just two aspects, divided many countries, especially Australia. It was as if we were fire ants or ticks, cane toads or the like who were unable to cross our own borders. All enforced by the state emergency services against their fellow citizens. That is a chapter in our history far greater than the vote on Indigenous executive rights. This was bound to fail, which it did with its sixty per cent No vote. From the Western World's perspective, as with the war in Vietnam, societal happenings were diligently reported through every conceivable modern communication.

We again relied upon scientists to develop vaccines – Astra Zeneca (UK), Pfizer (USA), MSD (USA) and others. Then in 2023 we were suddenly cured of the queues for blood tests and the like; Western leaders fell on their hypodermic syringe swords, but strangely not in the case of the dictatorships, such as China and Russia where, without democracy, one has no say.

As with previous pandemics, humanity has survived – easy to say after the event, on behalf of the now speechless casualties of Covid and, like wars before, now and in the future. Put simply, it did not have to happen, and we cannot do anything about it, with leaders cosying up to this super power on our doorstep.

With the end of the pandemic, the passenger planes emerged

from their desert graves to yet again drown out the barking dogs in the suburbs, and also the flying birds of natural origin. This was no easy task, with wind-blown sand occupying the seats of earlier paying passengers. Could things have been done better? We will never know within a world of interdependent divided societies.

Ukraine was opportunistically invaded by global thugs and the war continues as I write. War is now raging between Hamas and Israel. I have been to Israel (2019), so it is easy to imagine the horror occurring where the fighting is going on. Many years ago, I passed by Beirut in Lebanon and that country is now poised to attack. But as it risks retaliation from the US Mediterranean fleet that is currently a stalemate.

I suppose it is timely to write, rather than pontificate to dog walkers in the street, who really have no apparent interest in world affairs or what I may have done, or not done.

As I write, it is September 2023. In Brisbane, Australia. It is spring, though the leaves on the ground suggest otherwise. It is a subtropical spring, which is like no other. It is an island country of great size first inhabited eons ago long before early Dutch and Chinese explorers visited the west coast well ahead of Captain Cook and botanist Banks setting foot in Sydney in 1770.

The privilege of attending an exclusive GPS school lay in the origins of UK money left and used to pay the relatively expensive fees at the time to send a police officer's son to Brisbane Boys' College after attending Taringa State School. It was at BBC as a day boy among those of higher means that I passed through to Year twelve, starting in Year eight. Somehow, I managed to reach admission to the University of Queensland at the St Lucia campus, in Brisbane. BBC is a boarding school, so those who could afford it were mostly from the country – predominantly sons of cotton and sheep farmers. Australia was riding a wave of wealth, described as riding upon the Merino sheep's back.

My time at BBC will be mentioned and reflected upon later. Suffice to say that my son was school captain in 1991. His son, my grandson, likewise is at BBC. My daughter, Sara, attended its sister school, Somerville House, which is now attended by our granddaughter.

Now it is time to start at the beginning as best as my recollection allows.

Rod Hunt-Sharp
B. Pharm. ADSM. ANSM. M R Pharm. S . JP(CDec).

EARLY CHILDHOOD

I was born in Queensland on 12 March 1945 in a cottage hospital at Kilcoy, which was originally known as Hopetown, and as Hopetoun from 1904 to 1907. Its origins go back to the 1890s, with a pioneering school established in 1892. A hotel and a Church of England church followed closer to 1900. The hospital, known as St Margaret's, closed in 1946, the year after I was born.

My mother, Lillian Alma Hunt, and my police officer father, Albert James Sharp, had somehow met in the Caboolture area. Marriage soon followed and their first posting was to nearby Woodford.

Their first children, twins, were already six years old when I arrived, albeit with a few complications. Those who know me probably would say that a complicated birth would not be surprising as I can be a complicated person. Naturally I would disagree, but they are more than likely correct.

Woodford housed many US soldiers during the Second World War and my father witnessed many wartime incidents, including fighter planes crashing at the nearby Blackbutt Ranges. Inevitably the more gung-ho pilots smelt of alcohol as their planes burned around them. The coloured soldiers were separated and largely kept to themselves. A lot of local infrastructure was improved with American money, and my father told me it was the first time he had seen something called a biro (a ballpoint pen), from which ink was no longer spilt. The troops had a large canteen, where they wrote letters home using such pens. And they did not smudge, as they were largely waterproof.

My father was a strong and fearless man, with origins from the country. He was born in Toowoomba and had two brothers and two sisters. I did not see much of them in my formative years, which I regret and attribute to the dominance of my mother. There is a Charlmay Street along the scenic Prince Henry's Drive in Toowoomba named after my father's parents. Toowoomba is a lovely thriving city today, and I visited it many times in later years.

My mother was born in Canungra, to a father surnamed Hunt, who had emigrated from England as a schoolteacher, and a dominating mother, who was also a teacher. She had two sisters and two brothers: Harry Hunt, the elder brother, married into the Moon family; Ellie and Jesse, who never married; and Anne, who did marry – to Jimmie English. They lived in Charles Street, Caboolture, which is not far from Woodford and Kilcoy.

As I have had told to me by my late father, he came in to the birthing area where the doctor told him it had been a breached birth and that he was concentrating on saving my mother. My father enquired where I was, and having been told, 'over there', he found me unwrapped, probably crying and cold, with post-partum blood around and over me, which needed cleaning up. As he was quick tempered, I can only imagine what he said. I was quickly cleaned and wrapped up by a midwife, as the regular nurse was out of town. It might have been late at night – I just do not know – which could explain my predicament. I am pleased to say that the problem was obviously overcome.

I did not know it at the time but I already had a brother and sister, twins Nelson and Narelle, born in February 1939. My sister has often told me that when news of my birth arrived at the King Street house in Caboolture, my brother dived out of bed, taking a few curtains with him and was over the moon with excitement when he heard he had a younger brother.

All this was going on when the Second World War was coming to an end for US troops stationed around Woodford, a staging area ready to prevent the expected Japanese invasion to the north.

CABOOLTURE

I recall an old wicker pram under the Queenslander house at Caboolture, which no doubt served as an infant's form of transport. It was one of those cumbersome prams with a hatch-like roof, so to speak. I was told that it was a problem getting it past the cars parked under the house. My Uncle Jesse had a Ford Zephyr, which had to be backed out by the old tank stand to open the boot.

At this time when there was still a wait to be connected to the mains supply for tap water. Sewerage was a way off so toilets were in outhouses, affectionately called thunderboxes. The jerry can inside the hinged box upon which one deposited one's bum was collected by the dunny man and then rinsed out with a creosol disinfectant, usually by the householder. This prevented the growth of maggots from eggs laid by blowflies (blowies). Creosol (mind your hands) killed off this cycle to some extent. Having the outhouse situated down the back, for some sanitary odourless intent, was clearly not practical at night.

The fear of finding a black widow or redback spider under the seat was very real, and the inevitable spill of urine on the dunny's wooden floor made it quite rotten. Effluent from the round-handled black enamel containers, if overfull before the next dunny-man pick-up, made for useful fertiliser for the well-established fruit trees.

There was always sawdust from the Caboolture timber mill, which my uncle brought home on his bicycle. The car was for weekends and he much preferred to cycle to Attewell's Sawmill where, as a chartered accountant, he was the manager during the working week and loved and respected by all the staff.

Before the advent of the paper toilet roll, old newspapers were cut into squares, threaded with string and then hung in the dunny.

I was to become close to Uncle Jesse, who had great influence upon me whenever we met, which for many years was during the six-week state school holidays. He taught me self-reliance, by example and without uttering a word, other than to guide me forward.

I was not concerned with the delicacies of life as our family had struggled, although fortunately we had always been housed in government-owned houses. We had spent our Christmas holidays always at Caboolture, down and opposite side of Kings Street where Malaysian tin magnate, Mally Newman's huge home was, and not far from the Anglican church, where an eternal light hangs even today, to the memory of the Hunt family.

These were timber buildings. Brick ones were rare post war, particularly in this area. My mother worked as a bookkeeper at the Caboolture Co-op, where most of the farmers shopped and paid their credit accounts monthly. When adversity struck, such as wind-driven fires or floods, and their cash flow was reduced, she would extend credit for as long as possible to help them get by, which was the principle behind the Co-op's charter.

She got on well with the auditor from Taringa. It was unusual for a woman to have a job. Her brothers Harry and Jesse had gone to Brisbane Grammar School, where Harry had won academic prizes before going on to eventually become a manager with the Commonwealth Bank in Brisbane, which was on the corner opposite Wallace Bishop's jewellery shop.

Upstairs from there was a room where, for many years, Clinty Moon strung tennis rackets and was regarded as the one to get your Dunlop Maxply strung in natural catgut. Klipspringer was the best brand at the time and is still available.

It was a time when trams traversed Brisbane and when Nelson and Narelle (my twin brother and sister) were at Brisbane State High (a GPS school) and Uncle Harry met them at the tram stop. He would walk and talk with them to Central Station, where he saw them safely on the train for Sandgate. That was in the days of wooden rail carriages.

We were living at Sandgate after previously being at Edmonton, in the far north near Cairns. This was around 1955 and 1956. I was close to Uncle Jesse, the youngest of the Hunts in Caboolture, and we had a special affinity. He always kept a pressurised can of tennis balls in his car and one Christmas I was given a tennis ball on a string, which was pleasurable and very good for hand–eye coordination.

Christmas was steamy and hot, so different from England, from where their father (and his brother) had come as teachers. So to sit under the large mango tree near the outhouse (before septic was installed) was a cooling embrace. There was a swing, which we used, and we played tennis all day on the court. We had a mini golf putting range around the court and played table tennis under the Queenslander when it rained. Jesse had a high tank stand, which he had fashioned underneath into a shower. This was cold water from the rainwater tank above, and the croak of a green frog or two could be heard over the splashing water. Its coolness was bracing and invigorating at the same time; Lux soap and Johnson baby shampoo completed the military-like cleansing process.

Down the back past the orange and lemon trees and chook house, where fruit and eggs were in plentiful supply, was an old L-shaped air raid shelter which had been dug and sand-bagged and later filled in with old bottles, so I had been told. There was also a stile-like gate to the open fields towards the Caboolture River, where Jesse practised his beautiful golf drives. My father would have a go to see if he could hit a drive and hear the golf ball splash. Those that did not make it, we collected as we wandered down towards the river. It was a good area for flying a kite, bought at the same newsagent as the tennis balls. The kite always needed Tarzan's grip to stick the light balsa wood kite cross together before stretching the colourful fabric across when dry.

The Caboolture area is prone to storms and venomous snakes, predominately red-bellied blacks seen often lounging on non-submerged rocks in the water and the rocky bank near to where we swam. It was not polluted and we would also catch fish. Further upstream, garfish could be netted. We were taught to be aware of stonefish, because of their spiny sting. Crabbing was also done. Now all that is gone, and no one gives a damn (excuse the pun).

ROSEDALE

I was too young to recall accurately the earliest events after I was born. However, when just a young toddler, we moved to Rosedale near Bundaberg, after my father applied for a country posting as a married man with family. The powers that be at the Roma Street police headquarters placed him in charge of the Rosedale police district. It was largely a farming town, with a railway siding for loading beef cattle and receiving mail and parcels.

Fresh fruit was often parcelled in overnight from the north when floods did not prevent the trains from running, and from other areas, such as around Babinda and the Herbert River. That was during the wet season, which was often cyclonic.

A socially good time was had at Rosedale as it invited a village feel. On one occasion the Black Watch Pipe Band came from Scotland to play. The Anglican bishop came to town for christenings and confirmations when there were enough candidates. This created a frenzy to prepare a welcoming dinner for him. Often my mother played the piano at the local dance on a Saturday night in the local church hall. The farmers would dress up, awkwardly wearing ties and it would be a good night for all as I slept in a bassinet at the back of the stage. Perhaps the bachelors had the good fortune to meet a local girl, and whatever happened next, who will ever know?

It was always said that I never crawled and that I just got up and walked. Some also said that we had an infestation of ground fleas that needed the attention of flea powder spread about the typical Queensland Government-provided house. There was a concern that the welts on my skin and aggravated crying may have been from being bitten by them. Urban myth perhaps, but it was a time when DDT was still being used to spray for ticks on cattle and a low dose toxic flea powder contained probably the same chemicals if not worse.

The cattle were often sprayed as they went up the ramp into the cattle trucks. The smell of the cattle trucks on a hot day is something one does not forget. Yes, it is methane (CH_4) gas. There were always peewee birds that sat on the barbed wire fences, together with a variety of willy wagtails that darted on to the cows' rumps in a symbiotic gesture of tick removing. This is the antithesis of a sucker fish when clinging to a whale or shark.

My father was originally from the country, where he and other people on farms had suffered the Great Depression. This made for resilience and self-sufficiency and now especially so soon after the end of the war. In no time, up went the wire netting in the yard at the side of the police house to create a chicken house, using star pickets as uprights and fashioning some nesting areas in the ground.

For most of the children, this was a timely event. But not so for Narelle as she more likely knitted or played that game that uses an empty cotton reel. It was a time when toys were scarce and, even if available as they were in Bundaberg, we simply could not afford them.

All my life I was told that when I was born my parents only had sixpence in the bank. As I did not have much say in the event, I eventually let it go through to the keeper, a common phrase I was to use later in life.

Rosedale police station still had the wartime blackout tape on the windows. On the front fence a sign eventually went up saying people could pay or obtain SGIO there. This stood for the State Government Insurance Office, which had the ability to transact money to the CBA (Commonwealth Bank of Australia). Both were state and Commonwealth government-owned entities.

Dalgety's were the stock agents at the time. My father was good at recommending stock and life insurance. As a result, he earned some extra money for the family. At the time, he was struggling to give up cigarettes. He was always throwing the butts out the window from his office inside the house and retrieving them later. He would then roll up what precious tobacco was left.

Packet tobacco such as Ruby had a delicious smell and he supplemented the fresh with some of the old in a very cost-effective manner. No filter tip, just cigarette papers which he eventually lit with Redheads matches. It was his way of getting through the day. My mother was the housewife and we lived frugally. This was not by choice. It was a time when cakes and soft drinks were available, including Tristram's lemonade and orangeade soft drinks. There was also the now well-known Bundaberg ginger beer. Some people made their own alcoholic fermented ginger beer in their back garage. Sometimes the corks would burst before the use of snap-on lids came into vogue.

I recall the gleam in the eyes of my Uncle Jesse as he opened one and it sprayed everywhere. 'Too much yeast' he would dryly say through the dry ginger ale froth in his glass. Fermentation occurs when yeast is added.

My daughter took her young children, Jackson and Oscar, to Rosedale. Outside the fence was a driveway, which was not unusual. But what was unusual was that one day we children noticed that a speckled leaf vine growing wild on the ground had started to produce green elongated fruit. Our father assured us that it was like a small cucumber, which he said could be pickled. To remember that suggests it was a happy moment of discovery. Obviously, it had germinated from a seed from a previous fruit, washed into the ground by a few showers of rain. We later learned they were also known as gherkins – very tasty and eventually to become a big success in the fast-food world (as pickled cucumber) on McDonald's hamburgers and were probably already used with hot dogs in that far away city called New York.

As Rosedale was a fairly isolated place, our weekly or fortnightly grocery shopping was done in Bundaberg. This was an outing which always took the best part of a day, at that coastal largely Polish-settled country town. They had only one taxi, owned by a chap called Sankowski, of Polish stock. His pride and joy was an American Cadillac, which would take at least two car spaces to park. It was a very large car in Bundaberg, or anywhere for that time. It gleamed and glittered in the subtropical sun. Sankowski kept his pride and joy spotless.

It was a time when Elvis Presley sang on the airwaves, and other rock stars from the USA pounded their music into our ears. Johnny Cash was another. On the opposite scale were the crooners such as Perry Como and Frank Sinatra. Naturally there was the infiltration of the classics. Bundaberg had its own commercial licensed radio station, call sign 4BU.

The Bundaberg taxi service area started at the mouth of the Burnett River, followed the river upstream to Fairymead Road and then west to Hoods Road, Meadowvale Road and on to Heales Road. It then followed Heales Road south, Ten Mile Road and Manoo Road.

I have been told he was quite a character, dressing immaculately. No one knew much about him, dressed to perfection in a safari-type suit, but everyone knew him by his car, with white-walled tyres to match, as he stood by his beloved taxi in the main street of Bundaberg.

I can't confirm this, but he discussed cars, a lot, and in fact had some influence upon my father with the purchase of his first car. We clearly badly needed transport.

* * *

WELL, WHAT DOES A young boy like my brother Nelson want to do on a weekend? He must have heard from mates at the primary school about fishing at Baffle Creek. As it was not far away and a ferry was also there, such excitement had him pester Dad to go fishing there. To go fishing, first you have to have bait …

Agreement was reached that my father would show Nelson how to collect some bait. This meant getting some corn and meal from the chooks' feedbox and then acquiring a Tristram's wooden crate from under the house, which had yet to be taken back for more lemonade, sarsaparilla or orangeade. A forked stick and long string completed the basic trap. Crows were mostly caught. They were gutted with a small sharp knife, feathers flying out in a haphazard direction, as Nelson retrieved the innards. This was cheaper than going to the butcher for some offal even though it was the place to get old meat bones and scraps as the bones with a bit of rotting flesh after a day or so in the sun worked well in crab pots.

We also went yabbying in small creeks by dangling a string with meat tied to the end and a fish net to scoop them up. Boiled in briny water in a kerosene tin, they were every bit as delicious as a mud crab from Baffle Creek.

The Baffle Creek ferry was the primary means of transport between the town of Rosedale and the settlement of Baffle Creek. Baffle Creek was settled by German immigrants in 1908 and a ferry was established slightly downstream of the current site. A sugar mill was constructed on Wartburg Hill in 1911 and in 1915 the mill assumed control of the ferry, shifting it to its current location and constructing a new ferry.

We had a low-pressure weather event when we were there and a few tin roofs came off, so I was told when old enough to understand. An internet search for the second Rosedale police station shows the state school of today and many other buildings still standing as they did then.

There was a beef slaughtering house and a railway station at Lowmead, where no doubt cattle were offloaded, and we somehow acquired a poddy cow and a goat. They were train orphans, and my father was pleased to be given them by the stationmaster, since there were no claimants for them.

We had apparently advanced to having rolls of toilet paper in the community and this goat loved paper – so much so that the few times it was allowed to roam around the fenced police station, it would butt the dunny door open and go for the paper roll, pulling it outside from its cradle on the dunny's timber wall. Friendly goat horny nudges were not a good idea for a young tyke like me.

So my father talked to a nearby farmer who was willing to have the goat on the fenced paddock over the road. Sally, the poddy calf later joined it. My father often milked the calf, saying that the nutrients were good for a young child, for bone growth and the like.

It should be noted that this was not pasteurised milk, coming straight from the cow's udder to the kitchen table. Boiling then cooling before consumption should have sufficed, usually to kill off any TB bacteria. Without any proof, it was later thought that I had been infected at an early age. TB can lie dormant for years before flaring up after influenza, or any infection of the lungs which has lowered the body's resistance. Not much different from Covid except Covid is viral and TB is bacterial – a fact that took on greater significance these many years later.

EDMONTON

The state of Queensland is larger than many combined countries in Europe. It is bordered by the Coral Sea and the Pacific Ocean; to its north is the Torres Strait, separating the Australian mainland from Papua New Guinea, and the Gulf of Carpentaria to the north-west. Covering 1 852 642 square kilometres (715 309 sq. m), the state is the world's sixth-largest sub-national entity, larger than all but fifteen countries. It includes rainforests, rivers, coral reefs, mountain ranges and sandy beaches in its tropical and subtropical coastal regions, as well as deserts and savanna in the semi-arid and desert climatic regions of its interior.

We moved from Rosedale to Cairns with the prospect of a promotion, as the more country service one got the more one was likely to reach the rank of sergeant, or higher. Higher ranks were often a case of who you know, not what you know. Under the then premier there was much corruption – something I will say more about later.

It is important to state that my father was a fair man, an honest cop who went on to receive the Queen's Medal for Police Service, now even more prized with the passing of Elizabeth II. It is also prized because the Australian Labor Party is anti--monarchist resulting in orders and awards being changed from their former UK status to being Canberra-based awards. Thus MBE (Member of the British Empire) became OA (the Order of Australia) and so on. My brother received an MBE for pharmacy service, while the Westminster awards were still in place.

For many years, Vince Gair was the premier of Queensland, holding a majority of Labor members. Cairns had been historically always a Labor seat, and its member, Thomas Crowley, was born at Innisfail, the son of James Crowley and his wife Margaret (née Fitzgerald). He was educated at the Good Samaritan Convent in Innisfail and after leaving school was a wholesaler of wines, spirits and groceries in Cairns and a sugar cane and tobacco farmer at Mossman. He was State Parliament member for Cairns from 1947 to 1956, and previously a Cairns city councillor.

During that period 1953–56, my father was transferred as officer in charge of Edmonton, about seven miles south of Cairns, on the corner of Cattle Street, Edmonton, where a much more modern police station now exists. Ours was an identical footprint of some draughtsman drawings from the Public Service Works Department. It is noticeable that the updated steel and chain-wire fences have been retained.

The old Taringa police station still exists but the Taringa State School is sadly no longer. During visits to Cairns in 2018 (by ship) and again in October 2023, we were told that Edmonton was really now a suburb of Cairns, although the Hambledon Farmers' Co-op Sugar Mill was still there.

This was near the primary school I attended while with my brother and sister, being six years older, went to Gordonvale State School and high school. After a couple of years they passed their scholarship examinations and thence went to Cairns State High close by at St Angela's Convent.

Nelson had violin lessons and Narelle studied speech and deportment.

CAIRNS

Cairns State High School is the public-funded equivalent to Brisbane State High School – very good secondary schools that cost nothing in academic fees, as opposed to the Roman Catholic and other denominational schools such as Brisbane Grammar, Brisbane Boys' College, Somerville House, to name just those of consequence here.

Uncle Jesse and Harry Hunt both went to Brisbane Grammar School at a time when, in terms of years, distance and geography, coming from Caboolture was quite something. It was a time when it was unusual for an Anglican to be privately taught by Roman Catholic nuns. They reluctantly accepted Nelson, as he was left-handed, another sign of the times.

By coincidence, in October 2023, we visited St Monica's Church, which is in the vicinity of where they were taught. I enjoyed photographing the beautiful stained-glass windows. The Bishop's residence adjoining St Monica's was quite stately. But I will get back to that later as I have jumped the gun in this preamble.

I went to Hambledon State School when I was in grade one. It was a little way down the road from the police station towards Hambledon sugar mill. My brother and sister went to

Gordonvale High School for a couple of years. One day during a fete, Nelson, who was a good high jumper, was booed as a copper's son each time he was about to jump. Then the school bully knocked him down and pushed the high jump pole across his neck, with his go-to mates standing either side.

I was too small to do anything so watched helplessly as a teacher came to break it up but not before Nelson, using all his strength and choking for air, pushed away the pole and his attackers. It was probably Narelle who fetched the teacher as she was shepherding Nelson. The athletics fete continued with other country track and field events and I still recall the trees that provided welcome shade.

It was not long after this that they went to Cairns State High while I remained at Hambledon State.

* * *

UNTIL RELATIVELY RECENTLY ALL sugar cane, showing their flowering stalks, was burnt before harvesting by cane cutters – strong and tough hard-working men, mostly from Italy, contrary to the belief that only Kanaks were used. Nowadays the harvesting is mechanical.

At the Cairns Museum I was able to inform the volunteer guide that the cane cutters would live and die by their knives, as they cut the cane in the steamy humid heat. They also drank copious amounts of tea. Regardless of the burning of the sugar cane the cutters were often confronted with rats and python chasers, or just huge pythons that had consumed numerous rats.

They also had a canvas flask of water that evaporated through the canvas, which in turn cooled the water. We had one which we attached to the car, removing it from the front on dusty roads, and with a coat hanger hanging it on the window, on long road trips. Water is always precious.

My earlier mention of snakes being prevalent around Caboolture was an understatement compared to what was around in Cairns. There were blue tree pythons, and pythons were often regarded almost as pets in the sugar mills where they lived in the rafters above the crushers and burner.

The cane cutters started work early and rested during midday break, depending on how many sugarcane train trolleys they could fill. They were paid on the weight of cane cut or the number of trolleys filled. At the end of the day, they would go home and share an old Queenslander as a billet and get stuck into the gorgonzola cheese and a handful or more of green pickled olives from kerosene-can-size containers of imported olives, plus damper bread on the fire. They hitched a ride on the locomotive to save walking, and those white Europeans were so tanned they looked like they were from the West Indies. The most feared snakes were the coastal eastern brown and taipan, two of the world's deadliest.

* * *

AT CAIRNS POLICE STATION, there were some good times and some not so good. The age difference of six years with my brother and sister was becoming noticeable to me. I was not someone who would easily confide in people. I can't recall much about the state school. What I do recall were extreme events.

One was the Hambledon sugar mill fire.

Late one evening, our attention was drawn to a glow in the sky over to the west. We were soon startled to recognise whatever was happening was not far away. It needed investigation. We could smell the smoke and hear the sound of dry old timber exploding as it was licked by the flames of a massive and intense fire. With the smell of smoke and a hops-like flavour in the air, no second guesses were needed as to what was on fire. My fearless father was already in his khaki shorts and shirt with singlet, running down Cattle Street as a fire engine with bell ringing cruised by. He hitched a lift to the perimeter of the Hambledon sugar mill.

People are drawn to extreme events and it was not long before a crowd of locals, many employed at the mill, had gathered. My father took some civil control, and fire-fighters did their best. The explosions of sugar treacle being converted into molten toffee could be heard over everything else. Some people were concerned for the pythons in the rafters. But no doubt the pythons had slunk away at the first sign of something wrong.

The damage was repaired before the next crushing season, but rumours swirled around for years as to why the fire had occurred.

* * *

THE QUEENSLAND LAWN TENNIS Association (QLTA) had a tennis centre at Frew Park, Milton, close by the famed XXXX brewery. I played a lot of tennis there as I was growing up and the smell of hops always reminded me of that Hambledon mill fire.

I always smelt the Slazenger or Dunlop tennis balls when nervous. This reminded me of Uncle Jesse and helped me concentrate when playing tournaments. The tennis centre had a big wooden stadium that was the venue for Davis Cup matches. Sadly, it is all gone, due to the politics concerned with persistent flooding.

Over the years I progressed to become a Level 3 professional tennis coach – more of that later.

* * *

THERE ARE MEMORIES OF all the fun of the circus and country fair in Edmonton, named after a town in England. There is also one in Canada.

We always looked forward to the circus coming to town. I probably saw my first elephant and lion then. These were nomadic gypsy-like people. I doubt if it was Wirth's Circus, which was world famous at the time after having travelled to England. Circuses were popular and offshoots developed, with Ashton's being another I remember.

We played a game at the fair where we rolled a plastic disc down a grooved wooden incline hoping it would stop somewhere on the prize pad. With a little bit of rule-bending we would shorten the run distance from the top when the attendant was not watching and had significant success. Occasionally we may have placed a second disc on a square with a prize displayed, again without the attendant seeing. These were fun times in winning a treat.

We justified our actions because we were spending the money; and everyone winning a prize was the fairest possible excuse to counteract any question of our honesty. Our winning streaks were quickly curtailed when our parents found out. Their siblings blamed each other while I pleaded innocence and enjoyed scoffing down a Golden Rough. These were the most popular choice of prize, or else a small packet of Fantales (discontinued in 2023), Cherry Ripe and naturally Minties. It was like our own trick or treat, at a time when trick or treats were a long time from coming to Australia. There were the usual fairground rides as well.

* * *

BECAUSE SUMMERS ARE SO hot and humid in the far north tropics, winters seemed cold by comparison, when one became acclimatised. Influenza was present as were various tropical diseases. Many were transmitted to humans by mosquitos. Further north, in New Guinea, they also brought the malaria virus, and just about any virus was transported by the omnipresent flying foxes. They loved to feed on the Moreton Bay figs, with a wicked look upon their mammalian faces. They were also blamed for starting China's recent Covid pandemic from which humanity worldwide recently suffered. (I succumbed to it in Dunedin, New Zealand, in December 2022 while on a boat trip and it was still with us in 2023.)

I was probably around seven years old and running a fever when placed on a steel sprung bed on the veranda with a fan to help keep my temperature down. I remember being awakened by the presence of a burly apron-wearing home-care nurse towering over me. She was there to give me a look over and see why I had such a high fever as I had already been sick for at least a week.

Some rectally fashioned soap had already been tried to get me to defecate, but this had not worked. By mouth, I was given castor oil on a tablespoon – a very unpleasant way to overcome constipation. It made me vomit then and makes me feel like vomiting almost at the thought of it now. It was a case of hold your nose and gulp it down. Or have both neck glands pressed and nose held while one squirmed and spewed it up or down. Spilling some on my pyjama top meant smelling it for several hours as I drifted in and out of a delirious sleep.

Castor oil is a multipurpose vegetable oil that people have used for thousands of years. It's made by extracting oil from the seeds of the *Ricinus communis* plant. However, it did not work as there was still no joy of defecation.

Agarol, which is liquid paraffin emulsion with vanillin flavour, is the go-to today. Vanillin is an extract of the orchid. It is a precursor for other compounds in pharmacognosy and while synthetically available, the real deal is most flavoursome. It is native to Madagascar and is also grown in Indonesia and Mexico. I have seen it growing in India. Where would we be without a tub of vanilla ice-cream? We bought some at the supermarket and rushed it home with other food on very hot subtropical days. You might wish to tuck into some to continue with this narrative as you curl up on a winter's day in front of a hearth with a roaring natural fire.

*   *   *

SO WHAT IS DENGUE fever? Dengue (break-bone fever) is a viral infection that spreads from mosquitoes to people. It is more common in tropical and subtropical climates. That is what they thought I was suffering from.

Dengue is treated with paracetamol and there is no other specific treatment currently available. Usually, with a mild viral infection the viral disease is over in two weeks. Symptoms include swollen glands, pain behind the eyes, muscle and joint pains, nausea and vomiting (which would be enhanced by the thought of castor oil) and at times a noticeable rash. Daytime mosquitos are likely to transmit the viral disease, and the lifecycle of the virus has been widely researched to little effect regarding controlling the disease, especially in third-world countries.

There is a vaccine called dengvaxia, which is only suitable to some extent if someone has already had the fever. I believe it is a reportable disease, in urban areas in particular. Suntan lotion containing diethyltoluamide (DEET) is useful. The sun protection factor (SPF) of the suntan lotion reduces the risk of skin cancer and adding DEET inhibits the mosquitos.

It has been my observation that fewer people are using suntan lotion when they 'bake' in the sun. In the sixties, people were literally fried with spray-on coconut oil as used on the beach at Surfers Paradise in Queensland. The spray cooled the already burnt skin and the brain responded accordingly, until burning started again. Nowadays, long shirts and floppy hats are popular. Regardless of what manufacturers say, tanning lotions will wash off in the surf. (Coconut oil also forms part of those Golden Roughs mentioned earlier).

I am pleased to say that a sponge bath by the nurse and a dusting of Johnson's baby powder, especially to my lower back, became the norm for a while, together with a junket and jelly diet and ice-cream, and I gradually got stronger. Also I did so without getting those nasty bed sores, as they were known then, now described better as pressure sores.

When 'my bowels didn't work', an expression I detest, I was given an enema of warm soapy water. No Movicol or Durolax suppositories were then available. We did have the chocolate flavoured (senna) Laxettes, with dosage in squares. They were an excellent flavour follow up after the castor oil, helping to increase motility of the lower intestine. Senna has been around along with prunes since Roman times to treat constipation, or impacted faeces, depending on what you wish to call it.

I am pleased to say I survived, but the psychological scars of the trauma remain.

* * *

I REMEMBER AS A little boy being given a cowboy outfit, with riding pants and a six-shooter cap gun. I can still smell the cordite of the cap when it was struck with a blue-like flame as it went crack. This was the time of comic books and no television in the very hot and humid tropical north. Nor was there television in Brisbane until 1959, with the launch of QTQ Channel 9.

In Cairns, we relied on the radio with its call sign of 4CA, which remains the same today. I have never understood how licences are granted to various regions. Of course, there was the Australian Broadcasting Commission (ABC), which began in 1932 and added a television service in time for the 1956 Olympic Games in Melbourne.

So we had two radio frequencies, one commercial (4CA) and one government funded (ABC). My mother loved the ABC program *Blue Hills* (as did Aunty Ellie in Caboolture). This aired twice daily and was a drama series that, without competition, was nevertheless competitive. It had started as a social drama in 1949.

The ABC broadcast had a characteristic chime before a midday news bulletin. The local and a bit of overseas news kept us informed in the sweltering humid heat. Across the nation, mothers kept younger children entertained at home with *Kindergarten of the Air* and *Let's Join In*. The radio was in the kitchen, and looking out the shuttered window we noticed that the large tree was bearing a spiky round fruit. It looked like a konka, probably so named from the English horse chestnut or conker tree. We discovered what it was by asking some Chinese fettlers that it was a fruit tree.

On the other side of the house was another large tree which was bent over with a green to yellow fleshy fruit which eventually fell to the ground and provided a wonderful missile to throw at a wall to go *splat*! Their sugar content meant they fermented and rotted in the same way a mango does. A Chinese 'botanist' informed us it was a carambola or star fruit.

Apart from the cowboy suit, I also had a small tent, in which I role-played Buck Rogers or similar characters happily on my own. I would have had some help from my father, with a sigh, to erect it after Christmas in Caboolture. It was white with some Western bush ranger motif on one side. Thus, along with my sophisticated water pistol I was set to play for hours.

We were always wary of slithering nasties, though cane toads were fair game, especially if they were croaking in a downpipe. For some reason, unknown to me at the time, they (*Bufo marinus*) were not consumed by large pythons or taipans. Maybe it was something to do with their ugly appearance. Though I did know that if they got into a dog's water bowl, the dog could die from drinking the water.

Many years later I was to dissect a Queensland cane toad and give it drugs to test its nervous system response while studying first year zoology. However, green frogs were like caviar to one of these often-colourful reptilians. The dying croak of a green frog was regarded as an alert to the possibility of a snake's presence nearby.

One Saturday lunchtime during his daily routine of collecting eggs from our laying hens' nests my father suddenly yelled some expletives as he quickly exited the hen house, shutting the wire gate behind him and rushing to the toolshed. Hearing the commotion, I ran down the Queenslander's back steps. The clucking and squawking was followed by silence as our father,

Bert, stepped warily into the chook run with pitchfork in hand. Suddenly he stopped, raised the pitchfork with both hands above his head and thrust it hard down to drive it into a snake's squirming eleven-foot violently slithering body, just below its long angular brow.

He told the whole family peering through the chicken wire fence that he was sure it was a taipan. Along its body were three swollen bulbous areas. Its forked tongue shot out from its slimy scaly mouth, beneath eyes of black pupils and orange-brown irises. The underbelly was cream with orange spots and the normally slender body covered with tan-coloured scales. Its creamy writhing mouth held a very powerful venom which had already caused the death of some hens it had tried to swallow. Wet feathers around the hen's head told us the snake had tried to swallow it rather than just the eggs it had laid.

The venom is a neurotoxin with anticoagulant properties. It contains both haemotoxins (procoagulants), which affect clotting of the blood in various ways, and mycotoxins, affecting the muscles. The coastal taipan is extremely aggressive and fortunately an antivenom has been available since the mid-1950s. If bitten without being close to an antivenom, it takes around forty-five minutes for death to occur.

No doubt there were many unreported snakebite deaths among the early cane farmers, who were instead diagnosed with heart failure from heat stress as they lay in the fields, their black ash faces having turned bleached white as they lay lifeless among the sugar cane grass.

* * *

WHAT FOLLOWED THE KILLING of the taipan may be dismissed by some as an urban myth. But it is something I truly believe. I witnessed it; experienced it.

Word had got around about the larger than normal taipan, now pinned by its throat to our backyard. We were told not to go near it as it could still bite us. No touching whatsoever, as my father went on with his daily chores.

The venom gland of a taipan is behind its eye, with the hollowed-out injecting teeth angled backwards. When bitten, it is instinctive after the sudden prick to the flesh, to recoil away. It is a reflex action. But the backwards angle of the snake's teeth momentarily prevents this. In a nano second it injects the venom as its own nervous system reacts to the movement. Evolutionary speaking, these reptiles are obviously well adapted.

The Aborigines, who were friendly with Toby, our kelpie cross that we brought with us from Rosedale, told Bert, our father, that a Taipan will not die until the sun goes down.

This spooked the police station's young assistant probationary constable. He asked permission to use the station's Colt 45 rolling revolver and we watched with great anticipation as he pointed the gun at the snake's head. Not standing too close, and with limited firearm training, he pulled the trigger – and missed.

The dirt flew up as the bullet was embedded in the ground somewhere near the snake's head. The constable might well have been simply enjoying his moment of fun in the sun, although he purported to be serious. Either way, after a second shot echoed from the hills behind the Hambledon mill, my father emerged from behind his black Remington standard issue typewriter. He hurled expletives at the probationary copper and a spade was produced to cut off the snake's head.

Remember, this was in the 1950s and these were real dangers. Thus it was time to listen to the voice of the wise Aborigine elder, now peering at the dead reptile. It may well have been considered good tucker by their relatives in the non-urban areas.

To eat snake, one must remove the venomous head, cut open its long sinuous body and then skin it. It has a flavour like fish and is quite tasty. With added herbs and coconut milk on the side, one can survive in the bush or jungle. This is the way of life in South-East Asia and South America. Urbanised China sells pickled snakes, and snakes are an important part of Chinese medicine. Frying after scaling (like fish scaling) makes it nicely crispy. The flavour and texture resemble that of eel, which is particularly enjoyed in places that I have visited, such as Belgium, Vietnam and Japan.

The Aboriginal Elder, having mentioned the myth earlier, wandered by after closing time at the pub up the road. The sun was setting as he asked Bert about the snake. Toby, the kelpie cross, clearly knew him and no doubt had been fed meat pies by the Elder. His tail was wagging as my father ushered the Elder to the shot, pitchforked, very large and apparently lifeless Taipan.

My father had decided to burn it and called the probationary over to prepare to do this as the Elder peered down. His steely black eyes eventually met the hazel-blues of my father as he told him to wait until the sun went behind the hills. The probationary decided this was a joke. He pulled the pitchfork out and draped the snake around his neck.

The Elder had already stepped back from the stupidity he saw unfolding before him as the snake lashed out and, despite its broken spine, almost bit the constable. In fright, he dropped it. The snake aimlessly slithered a short distance away before stopping. The sun had just set and the Elder said approvingly he would take the taipan. He walked off with it around his neck, his jaunty gait clearly indicating his belief in the myth. After all he was staking his life on it.

Any fashionable ladies and gentlemen reading this should check the prices of snakeskin handbags, keyring holders, wallets and the like as they are quite expensive. The same goes for shoes. These items are mostly made from python leather. Vietnam is a good place to buy leather of this type. Some shops in Vietnam also have fine reasonably priced Italian soft leather, which is cheaper there than one would find at a roadside stall in Italy.

CHRISTMAS AT CABOOLTURE

As I mentioned earlier, we spent each Christmas down at Caboolture, near Brisbane, driving there in the Holden my father had bought and which he would service, himself, where possible. Come the start of school holidays we would head south – something we all looked forward to.

It was a long journey and this was in the early 1950s. Egyptians use a gourd for cooling water, which they sit with on the camels, as did the cane farmers of Queensland. It became a useful way to keep water cool in Australia in the 1950s and is still used with a no-frills canvas version costing around $300 in 2023.

My mother always had a siesta and had read somewhere, either in the *Women's Weekly* or perhaps the *Reader's Digest*, that putting water in a clean tomato sauce bottle and punching holes in the metal cap was a good way to keep cool when travelling. She was keen to try this and had a practice run in the house before collecting some bottles as the Christmas holidays loomed.

To have the sun beating down on the black Holden was a miserable experience by today's standards. There was no air conditioning although a vent could be activated by sliding a lever inside the car, which would raise a V-shaped meshed opening below the windscreen. There were no airbags for safety and seatbelts were being talked about as becoming mandatory. But when hot air was coming in and the vents became dusty insect traps, it was not that efficient. Vent windows at the front corner of the passenger's and driver's windows could be opened to deflect air in. Two teenagers and a youngie were in the back and the boot was packed. A rope tied around the non-recessed boot handle to part of the muffler made sure all was well fastened.

Before driving off on the two-day journey, my father and brother jumped up and pulled down fruit-laden branches of the lychee tree and put the fruit in the boot.

My parents set distance targets before stopping for a break and a Thermos flask of tea. The caffeine in the tea was to keep Bert awake, with sugar for energy as well. We always had handkerchiefs and sometimes small white face towels upon which mother would meticulously sprinkle the precious water. Often, it was sprinkled straight upon one's head as we bumped along. The water would evaporate and cool as we opened the hankie and it was not uncommon, when the roads were not too dusty, to let a towel flap in the wind to evaporate and cool. This would either be placed on the forehead or tied in a V around the neck, which later became fashionable on tennis courts. Prominent examples of this were stars such as Laver, Emerson, Hewett and Stolle. Laver – the 'Rockhampton Rocket' – was probably the best in his era and certainly the winner of the most Grand Slams. Ant hill bed courts were a feature of many parts of Queensland and the outback and were where Laver learned to play the game that brought him worldwide fame.

As Laver writes in *The Education of a Tennis Player*, 'My first court was ant bed, homemade by my dad and the boys in the family. It's common stuff in the Australian Outback. You knock over an anthill, which has become quite hard, crush it and spread the grit on a level piece of ground where the grass has been skinned off. It plays a lot like clay.'

* * *

IMAGINE DRINKING WATER FROM a gourd, which had gone through sandy clay roads, with the condensation dripping with clay and splattering the shoulder of the road as it was decanted into a clean Thermos flask. 'A little bit of clay never hurt anyone,' father would say as crows squawked and we ate our ham sandwiches in the car.

There were always a few toilet rolls on board for use after stopping to find a tree. In those days, urinating against the rear back tyre was legal. It was easier for males. However, anyone choosing to squat near or over a buzzing mound of green ants had to look out for a very nasty bite on the bum.

Those ants had a warped sense of adventure; they would quietly climb up your leg, under any loose-fitting pants, and then bloody bite you.

There was always the worry of an unwary snake slipping into the engine mounting, only to later suddenly pop up outside on the window. Worse, if it found its way up the clutch well and on to the floor near one's feet! As I recall, this did not happen to us; but it did happen to others.

This was all in addition to terrible roads, which still need continual repair in 2023. Mind you, most are sealed these days; so one only has to dodge the potholes.

Then there were the large cattle trucks that would overtake or pass from the opposite direction, causing a temporary dust storm. The dust taste tickled all the senses. This was the faster inland route, which is now called the Great Inland Way.

* * *

ONE RETURN TRIP FROM Caboolture is forever etched on my mind's eye.

It was dusk and raining heavily, with only one of the Holden's windscreen wipers working. As we rounded a bend in the road father quickly applied the brakes – and nothing happened. In front of us out in the middle of the road, and with the Herbert River road bridge just beyond them, were people frantically waving warning torchlights.

The brake pedal sank to the floor and father quickly shifted down through the gears to slow the car. We began skidding and the car's lights lit up some dark ghostly figures, jumping up and down, with hands held up and palms facing us in the classic *stop* sign. Then we all saw why and what was happening. The Herbert River road bridge was nowhere to be seen.

Our speed had reduced but we were still inching towards the figures and the raging flooded Herbert River. I recall, with handbrake on, my father opened his door and put his sandshoe-covered right foot outside on the wet bitumen road. Imagine doing a clutch start when a manual car's battery has failed. It was like that. But still we kept sliding as the group of torch wavers came closer and closer to the car. It all happened so fast, it was hard to fully appreciate the bravery they had shown by putting their bodies on the line to stop the car. These mostly Indigenous men had saved us from a certain drowning.

Archival February weather records show there was heavy rain on the far north coast during the first twelve days of the month, when totals up to 1125 mm were recorded, disrupting rail, road and air traffic and culminating in serious flooding of the low-lying areas in the Herbert River basin on February 12.

We all piled out of the car, and my father, with the help of others, placed large rocks in front of the rear and front wheels. The bonnet felt warm, the rain was splashing on us and the car became steamy from the body and bonnet heat. It rolled off like a melting ice-cream down its cone. All this was aided by the intense humidity of early February, and we were thankful to these people that we were alive.

The Herbert River had stopped our forward advance, which meant we still had around 200 km to travel to Edmonton, which nowadays is a popular place for canoeists to shoot the rapids, with a water system rivalling that of the Franklin River in Tasmania.

So we had to make other arrangements to get back to work and school, and the only option was to go by train, provided the trains were operating.

* * *

DIESEL–ELECTRIC ENGINES HAD BEEN imported from England and the construction of train carriages was at Ipswich near Brisbane. I was always fascinated to see a Garratt steam engine pulling a train. It looked so very sleek and modern.

We had to backtrack to the nearest 'city' with a railway station served by trains which would transport us to Cairns. However, the train lines were also washed out and bridges damaged (as with the roads), which made them impassable. They all had to be repaired, and that takes time for such infrastructure. We therefore rented a house at a place called Cardwell until the trains started running again and we could leave this substandard accommodation and start heading home.

I remember little except that it was a prominent high-set house, owned by the state government (probably a police house or associated works department). It had not mattered at the time as we were stranded and were lucky to have a roof over our head. The plan was to get back by rail, and decide what to do about Betsy the Holden.

My father managed to have it rail freighted, which was not uncommon in those days and not unlike the military trains we see on the television moving from Russia to Ukraine.

After a few days we were set to go, out of pocket and a little tense, as we boarded a wooden carriage made of Queensland timbers and with leather seats. Not quite the Orient Express or the Eurostar, but to my surprise, as we rumbled along we were shown to a dining car and I remember well my first meal on a train. It was roast beef and roast vegetables with lovely gravy. Wow, this was special. Then it happened …

I choked on a piece of gristle which had lodged in my oesophagus or throat but, either way, it set off a panic attack as I struggled to breathe. I was told to try a finger or two to grab it. No joy. Then someone thought they would slap my back, which startled my senses. Eventually it was retrieved and the long stringy bit with a string bean or bit of carrot was deposited on a waiting serviette. The psychological after-effects lasted many years. That I can still remember it is a testament to that.

It was not a good end to that year's Christmas at Caboolture. Most of our time there consisted of playing tennis all day long in the heat of summer. In the beginning, I had to take a back seat as I was still learning. Uncle Jesse was so patient; he always gave me a hit at the end of each set whilst the others rested. Lunch was usually ham, or cheese, tomato and homemade pickles or mango chutney. Aunt Ellie was a keen cook and also an avid grower of orchids. The orchids were magnificent when in bloom enclosed in the black-sheeted area she had set aside for them.

For a while, near the start of the clothesline to the left of the then ant bed tennis court, was a copper, the forerunner of today's washing machines. A wood fire was kept alight continuously under the copper, with occasional stoking. A stick was used to stir heavy linens and cottons when they were in the boiling water. Often the heavy bedsheets were scrubbed with brushes every thirty minutes or so. Nowadays, a good washing machine such as a Miele or Bosch does this at the push of button.

Uncle Jesse saw another use for the copper.

He moved it out of the wash shed area underneath the Queenslander to near the angled forked wooden-supported washing line. His reasoning was that it would be useful for slow cooking of meats such as salted beef. This was a cheap cut in those days and my father, when we lived at St Lucia in Brisbane, used to regularly do the same with salted beef bought from the butcher down the road. The beef would be rolled and strung and injected with a brine solution by the butcher with much applomb.

My father usually dropped some whole onions and herbs into the boiling water. Served on a slice of bread with some Keen's mustard or chutney, it was delicious. We also found it popular when we visited Washington, USA, although I must say, that one must have had some mustard and cardamon seeds thrown in as well.

With the flames licking up the side of the copper, the salty solution would come to the boil. A full leg of ham, held by a strong tie of clean twine to the washing wood stirrer stick and rubbed with salt, would be dropped into the boiling water. Some cloves would be sprinkled in with a few more later stuck into the softened skin. Orange marmalade drizzled over the joint when cooked and cooling worked a treat. The mix of sweet and sour flavours is always good. The cooking time was determined by experience, depending on the size of the ham and how many were going to sit down at that Christmas feast accompanied by bonbons, dad jokes and trinkets.

A self-closing screen door at the back steps between the dining room and kitchen allowed air to flow through the central corridor of the Queenslander house. As it was built on stilts breezes flowed underneath. There a couple of cars were parked end to end, and a table tennis table rested on its side, ready to be put on carpenter's trestles for a game. The trestles were held by rope to prevent them collapsing. Sandpaper-covered Szabados bats – named after Australian table tennis champion Miklos Szabados – were stored high on the edge of the house stump, and in a chest of drawers was a box of table tennis balls.

The odd shuttlecock would be rolling around as well as a couple of boxes of golf balls, some used and others with their wrappers still on, and, most importantly, some tennis balls in a string bag. The new balls were always under the seat of the Zephyr. For a while there was a transition from a box of around twelve white tennis balls to the pressure cans, which are used today. These are opened a few minutes before use to limit the effects of the pressure. Yellow balls were developed and the better ones were Dunlop or Slazenger, whereas Spalding was more into squash and basketball. Slazenger's wooden tennis racquet was popular, as was the Dunlop Maxply once Dunlop sorted out the fracturing of the throat with use. Before the advent of the synthetic strings, catgut was used. This presented a problem during the wet season as then a broken string was more likely. Stringing a racquet took time and the spare racquet for everone to use was never as good. It was also a time when racquets were firmly held in a vice or protector 'press' to prevent them warping. Shellac was used as a coating aganst the wet for the strings.

The large leg of ham from the local butcher, cooked in this way, was absolutely delicious. But the coup de grâce was the plum pudding, which had earlier been cooked in the copper using a calico-bound mixture of Ellie's recipe. The brandy flame ceremony would precede the adding of custard and vanilla ice-cream to this delicious sweet. Breakfast the next day was always ham, poached eggs and toast, with liberal amounts of tomato sauce.

Presents were usually opened first up in the morning, over a cup of tea and mince pies. There were inevitably copious numbers of Christmas cards on display on the sideboard. Crimple-cut coloured paper was strung from the ceiling and the nicely decorated and freshly cut pine tree was at the far end of the dining room. Curious young eyes had checked out the presents after we arrived around the week before Christmas.

There was always a big letdown after Christmas, and eventually my mother got itchy feet, keen to get back home. My father felt the same.

CORRUPTION, TENNIS AND MUSIC

My father was disgusted with the extent of corruption in the police, but especially with respect to illegal bookies. These SP (starting price) bookmakers were not registered and provided kickbacks to those police who turned a blind eye. The saying that 'when the fish dies, it rots from the head first' was one way to describe it.

One day, my mother answered an unexpected knock on the door. To her disbelief a member of parliament and a police inspector were standing there. They said they had stopped by to say hello and made small talk about how much we were respected for our convictions (excuse the deliberate pun). They came in for a cuppa and after settling in, opened a briefcase full of cash.

They offered it to my mother. Bert did not need to know about it, they said, and she could have these few thousand pounds. The only condition was that she stopped my father raiding and charging the corrupt SP bookies. She refused.

My father agreed that this was a matter of disbelief, although they both saw it would be a way to afford the children's education back in Brisbane.

Needless to say, it was not long before my father's application for transfer back to Brisbane was approved, as the powers that be were happy to get rid of a straight cop who spilled the beans.

There was a lot of corrupt under-the-table money at stake. One individual was still remembered on a recent visit to Cairns, when I had a chance conversation with a retired copper's son at a model village shop.

However, the move was not made straightforward for us. Instead of a station posting with house, we were given accommodation in a dilapidated old house within the Brisbane Valley tram depot. It was already probably fifty years old and surrounded by the sounds of clinking electricity-flashing trams as they came and went from the depot.

My father had been transferred to Roma Street, without promotion. You didn't get a promotion then or now, I suppose, if you spill the beans. This was before an effective police union existed. If you did not fall into line with the commissioner and his assistants, you were not well tolerated.

Later, there was the Whisky-A-Go-Go nightclub fire in the Valley and one or two police commissioners were later investigated. Readily available extracts from the subsequent Fitzgerald Enquiry explain the corruption in much greater detail. The corruption in Cairns was clearly endemic. However, as Cairns was a long way from Brisbane it was brushed under the carpet, so as to speak. (Hear no evil, see no evil.)

* * *

AUNTY MABEL AND UNCLE Charley Jessen were first cousins

or second – I never knew exactly what they were to my mother. They were elderly and lived at Shorncliffe near Sandgate, which had a rail connection to the Valley, Roma Street and Brisbane Central. So it was with a feeling of gratitude that they welcomed us to stay.

It also meant that Nelson and Narelle could travel to Brisbane State High, transferring their enrolment from Cairns State High. (My parents had looked at BGS and BGGS, which they could have attended, but the subject choices were better at BSHS.)

This was conveniently forgotten, resulting in some derision towards me for many years when I went to the private school, Brisbane Boys' College.

While at Shorncliffe I was enrolled mid-year as a primary state school student. Some sort of poxy school uniform of KingGee pants and shirt, with a splash of colour on the short-sleeved shirt, and black shoes were the recommendations. It had a tennis court, where extra coaching was available if your parents paid the substantial additional fee.

I absolutely detested the place. Kids arrived without shoes and there was the usual bullying. I remember that on one occasion when I refused to go my father picked me up, smacked me very hard, pulled me into the car, drove me to school and took me in to the class teacher. Yes, he was in uniform, which was about the last straw! Later, the bullies started up in the usual fashion of the period.

I did get friendly with a John D....who was a very good competitive tennis player. I remember him blowing his green slimy snot on to his finger and with a pleased smile on his dial, then wiping it on a brick wall. Nice, and typical of this auburn-haired 'wealthy son' of a Shorncliffe realtor.

He wanted me to come and play with him on their ant bed backyard tennis court. But, no, I was not allowed. He and other people were to become adversaries later on when I played in the Queensland state age tennis tournaments. Many had the benefit of tennis practice at home; others were sons and daughters of coaches who had tennis centres. I was to eventually meet them all.

Tennis, as a sport, is tough. Without opportunity and a great deal of practice, competitively you are out before you start. To make it on the circuit, as it is now known, you have to have an immense talent, plus the psychology of self-belief. Of course, this does reflect on one's general later life skills. This was the time when Rod Laver, 'that guy from Rockhampton', was making his presence known. I have never seen a backhand topspin drive quite like the one he had, and I have seen and coached extensively.

One thing I must mention is the degree of physical fitness needed. As I type this, I am painfully aware of the damage to my rotator cuffs. Yes, it is an age factor, but people age more physically the more active they are. The type of sport played can be directly correlated to later life medical results. Good examples are boxing and contact sports such as rugby. Swimming, not unlike tennis, generally stuffs up the rotator cuff.

Generally speaking, they were fairly happy times, including borrowing my brother's air gun and shooting pigeons under the mango tree. No one wanted to eat the squabs as they were not the ordinary common worm-ridden city pigeons. They had a top to them so we called them top-notched pigeons. More accurately, they were crested pigeons. Rarely there were also bronze-winged pigeons. The trick was to get close for a shot, slowly squeeze the trigger, and the air through the Singer sewing machine oiled barrel would spit life to cause death. To wing them with a shot was to have no lead shot in the plump belly to remove.

I must have read about all this to act it out on a Saturday afternoon. My favourite books were by Enid Blyton and the Biggles books were also great. I had pen pals overseas, one in the USA and one in the UK. Correspondence was only every few months because of the cost of postage. Eventually, aerogrammes emerged, which were much less expensive.

Yes, happy days. But time marches on and it was soon a time to leave that behind.

SHORNCLIFFE AND BEYOND

From an early age it was clear that though I was outwardly quite shy, inside I was boiling over with enthusiasm to do something interesting with my life. While living at Shorncliffe I sat many times with Mabel and listened to her play the piano. I loved the music and made the mistake of saying so.

I had never seen a metronome, though Mabel had already explained it before I had my first lesson. She encouraged me to wind it up, which I hesitantly did. I did not wish to overwind as you could with a clock. Sitting next to her on the piano stool was not the most comfortable place to learn as the freshly wound metronome ticked away. Nowadays, to use the phrase *tick tock* in describing the workings of a metronome immediately conjures up some app, or computer application, which mysteriously finds its way onto one's mobile phone.

Mabel talked endlessly about her love for England. Husband Charlie was Australian, though he claimed some ancient ancestry to Scotland. I don't think he ever worked and, to be honest, I think that when we paid and stayed, it was useful money to top up their pensions.

Slim with white flowing hair and a moustache tainted brown

on the edges from tobacco, he loved Saturday afternoons. This was his moment to see if he had backed a winner at the races. He rolled his own cigarettes and was happy as Larry out the back, in his large chair, listening to race day on his transistor radio.

I did not have the patience or time to stay cooped up inside a house while learning music. Imagining myself as a developing musician such as John Hunt, a London concert pianist of note, who Mabel said I resembled, simply didn't cut the mustard at that early time in life. Subconsciously, I was becoming attuned to a desire to travel, to see and meet all the people Mabel mentioned as my relatives, whether they were a second cousin or not.

She raved so much about how I looked like John Hunt that it became engraved on the inner sanctums of my mind. Then there was a Lady Simon, wife of Lord Simon, who was chairman of P&O London. She showed me (indeed showed the whole family) photos of them at the Waldorf Astoria in New York, and various other photos she had received. I felt they must have had quite a rapport for her to be receiving all these photos.

At Christmas, Mabel would send us a Christmas cake across by parcel post from the GPO (General Post Office) as it was then known. Later I was given some records by John Hunt, and on her death years later at the nearby Eventide Home we came across her piano. Strangely, my brother became trustee of the estate. But what happened to the old house was something I was not privy to.

Lady and Lord Simon visited Brisbane in the early sixties, staying at the Park Hotel down by the Brisbane Botanic Gardens.

That was the place to stay at that time, with the Hilton Hotel still to be opened. John McEnroe stayed there many times and relaxed by throwing frisbees in the park. Koalas were brought to dignitaries for photoshoots and subsequent publication in the *Courier Mail*.

Brisbane was a small country city then and as far as I am concerned it still is in 2023. But it is a liveable place with a delightful subtropical climate and set in a democracy, isolated for now from those who wish ill upon us.

* * *

BRISBANE IS DOMINATED BY the Brisbane River, and only really began to be noticed on the world stage when the World Expo was held there in September and October 1988. Previous to this, there had only been the 1982 Commonwealth Games – an event we had a bit to do with, which I will discuss later.

Another World Expo is to be held in Riyadh in 2030, which readers may fancy flying and possibly camelling to. As it is an Arab nation, this would really be something worth seeing. I love their architecture, which is a blend of old and new. There is nothing like seeing a whitewashed mudbrick building in the backstreets of any Middle Eastern city. It's the cool smell inside that greets one upon entering. Then there is the smell of Middle Eastern tobacco that taints the air and, depending on where you are, the aroma of fresh spices on sale in open-air markets.

This mixture heightens the senses, within an ancient tradition. Copious amounts of myrrh still engage the curiosity of the traveller. It is an ancient kingdom where you can be lost in your thoughts. Different class structures exist side by side, and the leaders have yachts of a size that is hard to believe.

Beautiful olive-skinned people adorn the decks of these yachts in their Gucci bikinis and sunglasses to match. Doubtless several more of each plus outfits and shoes would be stored in their luxurious guest cabins. These are people with wealth, on show within some sort of democracy, helped by the omnipresent USA playing the role of policeman to the world.

* * *

SHORNCLIFFE HAS A PIER from where the Brisbane to Gladstone yacht race starts. I have never seen it; though it is seen as a precursor to the world-renowned Sydney to Hobart race starting in Sydney on Boxing Day. These yachts are also the domain of the wealthy, and I did witness the latter race coming into Hobart while on board a boat cruise a little while ago.

I recall swimming near the pier and well remember asking my father the cause of the nibbles and jumping we felt as we splashed. Father was a good swimmer but my mother never went into the water. Narelle was pretty much the same; Nelson, being six years older and more outgoing than me, took off on his own at every opportunity.

It was high tide and the water was murky. The gentle lapping of the waves against the pier's oyster and barnacle-encrusted struts was the only thing that fractured the stillness of the morning. There were sea lice, and the occasional jellyfish and bluebottle to negotiate as I lunged forward and caught in my cupped hand one of these jumping creatures. They were banana prawns, delicious when cooked and eaten with vinegar and thousand island dressing.

It was probably around then that I was told to treat jellyfish stings by rubbing sand into the affected area. Antihistamine steroidal cream would have been better though, if it was available. I was not to learn about that until many years later.

Around the coast from the pier is the tidal Breakfast Creek. Even today, this is the place to buy fresh seafood directly from trawlers who net the waters of Moreton Bay and beyond. They tie up near Sinbad Street, Shorncliffe.

During a friendship of many years – which waned with time and innuendo – I went down there to buy seafood. I liked it and my friend preferred beer as well. Fresh crusty bread and thousand island dressing or white vinegar made for a yummy meal. Lettuce salad optional.

* * *

MY FATHER WAS UNEXPECTEDLY called into the Roma Street inspector's office to be told that his application to be officer in charge of Taringa police station had been successful and he would be appointed shortly.

This meant we would all be moving from Sandgate to the rent-free house with a new school for me, and Narelle and Nelson could still travel to BSHS on the train from the Taringa station.

The Taringa police house is still there today but what it is used for is unknown to me. I was to revisit it many years later when I was a pharmacist. That was when they had officious CIB detectives there. The good news was that on the other side of the zebra crossing was Taringa State School, with more than seven hundred students from year one to scholarship year.

Morrow Street is the road that runs up the hill from Moggill Road, which splits at the bottom. Hungry Jacks is still there and a homeless person named Ziggy lives in the tiny park below the medical centre.

This is close to the former championship-size tennis courts at the former Taringa State School. Opened in 1900, it was gone in 1996. Not a chance to wait for an extra four years for the centennial year, when the government no doubt raised funds by the property's sale for overseas student accommodation. Who is the overall owner? How do you rent one? It is all a mystery to me and if the reader has detected a cynicism towards inept governments, then that is a fair call.

Over the years, both sides of government in Queensland have been appalling. None of them can claim any sense of achievement without acknowledging the lack of fair and equitable stewardship as elected leaders. Unfortunately, this is not unique to Queensland.

* * *

THE MOVE WAS MADE and it was not long before the youngest son had his enrolment interview at TSS. It was a formality.

Somehow my father agreed to be lollipop cop for the morning car and pedestrian arrivals. This was great as I made my way to school by crossing the road with his help. However, I soon became aware of the whispers – 'Hey, that new student is the copper's son' – that made me the subject of derision and the usual bullying began. What irony that those student hostels where the school once stood are now full of overseas students. Was it some quirk of fate?

When I was at the Taringa school there were a few immigrants from Europe. I recall a gentle giant of a British student being in a fight with a Australian student. 'Pommie bastard' was bandied about along with punches, and the smaller fellow won the day with a nosebleed to the gentle giant. I watched this sickening display, with the sound of flesh upon flesh and the inevitable red blood. Oh!

Also well remembered is the free milk provided daily. Free milk? Yes, free milk! Several crates were delivered to most of those at school. There was no lactose intolerance then. This was postwar and the decision to provide free milk most probably stemmed from some minister visiting Queensland House in London and hearing this happened in the UK. Such was his fact finding that near election time this was something electorally pleasing to introduce. Naturally it was his idea.

By the way, there were no women in Parliament then. So, what was the caper? Well, some smarty would at lunchtime pour all the dregs from the empty (half-pint or perhaps they were a quarter) glass bottles in the crates into one bottle. After carefully re-sealing the silver cap it looked like the real deal. Brushing away the flies and the smell of the now-sour milk, it would be offered to an unsuspecting person.

After they had consumed this bonus somewhat hastily, the victim (he or she) would be told the true story. This caper was a regular occurrence until they were caught out. After that a milk monitor student would be responsible for washing empty bottles in the storage crates. Put simply, when finished we washed them in the drinking troughs before placing them back in the crates. Thus, a little bit of individual responsibility overcame the little pricks who abused civility. Probably, if it was done to them, they would burst into tears.

Taringa State School had no swimming pool, so pupils were taken by train or bus to the nearest state school for lessons. I could not swim as a result of my mother's dominating controlling nature. She had a thing about drowning and lack of supervision; so a note was written to the school. This meant staying behind with a couple of other students at school for supervisory studies.

One teacher was a Mrs McGucken. I didn't know then how to describe it but relatively recently a physiotherapist described obese women with a hip failing as doing a duck waddle. In any recollection of this grumpy person I would be describing her similarly. I remember her threatening to hit me across the knuckles with a ruler because I cut something crookedly. I replied that the scissors were blunt, which made her breasts heave with anger.

Teachers were totally boring to me. Inwardly I detested authority while accepting where I was situated at the time. Perhaps that means having a lot of patience? However, anyone who knows me will quickly argue against that. But generally I got by with the ability to offer a quick response.

However, there was one teacher who was exceptionally good. The last year of primary school was called the scholarship year. Parents then, as now, get a feel for good and bad teachers. This man of Irish descent who I was fortunate to have in scholarship year was Mr Eugene O'Shea.

Some people are born to be teachers, others are simply lazy with no idea of how to communicate. The latter were more often to be found in grades one and two on the long haul of the education spectrum. They had their little pet students, and cakes and chocolate fattened up the already dumpy-do lazy teacher. There were exceptions, and some very good (by comparison) teachers were there. If they were career minded the good ones often found their way into better-paid positions in private schools. It was also an age when females tended to choose between a career and being a housewife. Nowadays there is a compromise which is complicated to describe, except to say things have improved for married teachers.

I stand to be corrected, but I believe along with thousands of other primary school students I actually sat for the last scholarship examination held in Queensland. It was late in the year of 1957 that I sat this at Taringa State School. In the last year of school we actually had home rooms for classes and had been graded by academic ability. I suspect the teachers looked over the lists and the most senior teacher got to choose from the list the class he wanted.

This was a significant examination as it helped determine a student's ability to progress in the education system. We were marked externally by teachers at other schools. As a result of the exam some people were steered towards careers in a trade and others were encouraged to continue their education at a secondary school. State government secondary schools were simply the pits, with a few established exceptions (Kelvin Grove and BSHS, CSH et al). This came at a time when there was a noticeable increase in development of religious dominated private schools.

The Catholic Church schools thrived as the fees were very low, and the word around the household kitchens was that they were heavily subsidised by the church. For the really wealthy students, some private schools were already offering limited primary education, and others were including boarding opportunities. These are now very big business.

The private denominational schools of all faiths, such as Jewish (mostly Melbourne) and Islamic (Sydney, Melbourne, Brisbane) are in the mix. During the seventh century Muslims developed madrasas for those Muslims who wanted a religious education. So history does repeat itself in denominational education. It is much more sophisticated now and no doubt hard to imagine where it will go.

* * *

CALLING SOMEONE OUT MEANT conflict and I saw enough conflict at home. In a sense I was worse off than an only child because I had two older siblings who could knock me around due to their age advantage of six years. As they were twins, they had a natural affinity to gang up as a supportive team against me when necessary. There were lasting effects from that time, and it continued to be the same in later years.

We seldom talk these days. If I was willing to be the conduit for conversation between them, well that would be fine. These days I would only do that in an emergency.

However, when the chips are down they are reliable. I would say my brother would lead with reliable emotional support in matters of health, but if it were a monetary matter that is another story, which is fair enough; but I do not think I am like that, probably being generous to a fault.

I had a friend called Andrew who was an only child and someone to see on weekends when both of us were free. He used to come around on Saturday mornings when the baking was on in the kitchen. Like all of us he enjoyed Narelle's jam drops.

We would make our way down the hall towards the baking fragrance coming from the old stove in the kitchen. He lived across the tracks and up the hill in a Queenslander. His mum was tall, and so was he. His father had a nice Volvo car of the period shaped like a cane toad. He sold furniture at a wholesaler's store near the Regatta Hotel on Coronation Drive.

* * *

As I remarked earlier, Eugene O'Shea was a very good teacher to have in scholarship year for important subjects such as maths and English. It was he who took the last year class for primary maths and English, while someone else took geography and history and perhaps limited chemistry, depending on subject's chosen.

The only time another student physically hit me was when walking up the steps to class and this fellow, called Toby and known as the bully of the year, suddenly produced a right cross punch to my cheek.

I was stunned as I was not expecting it and also because it had a bit of force behind it. It was unprovoked. Being on the receiving end was something that I was unable to digest. What was the reason for it?

I am not sure what happened next but, unknown to me, Mr O'Shea was by now looking down from the landing above – clearly a bad moment to retaliate. With his good view of fellow students marching up to class, my timing was not the best. I simply took the bully's feet out from under him with a quick clip to his heels. The whimpering little creep was soon displaying his true character, as he struggled to his feet at the bottom of the stairs. As the uninjured creep scampered to Sir for protection, a deep booming voice yelled at me like a clap of thunder. I had to report to the classroom at lunchtime. I fully expected cuts were to follow, as it was a time when caning still occurred. I resolved not to tell my parents.

After Mr O'Shea asked me what had happened, and I had told the true story, I was not to escape disciplinary measures. I was not caned but was given extra work to do in the lunch hours. The bully got off scot-free as I took the blame for only what Mr O'Shea could see. Only the bully's pride had been blemished. I was pleased I had stood up to him, as were others. He had been made to look so awkward and clumsy when on the receiving end – such a distinct contrast from getting away with dishing it out with cheap shots, like that right cross.

The punishment was an excellent opportunity to ask subject questions of Mr O'Shea and so revise for the coming scholarship examinations. I had to explain this lunchtime activity to my parents as an additional learning and revision opportunity because during lunch hours I was expected to keep in touch as our house was just across the road from the school.

This tight parental control was feeding a suppressed psychological anger within myself, which I failed to realise until much older.

The night and day before each examination subject was spent studying with my mother checking my arithmetic (mathematics as a beginning), geography and the like. As I sat down to the folded exam paper on the desk at Taringa School, I knew this was it. A make-or-break situation.

It is always good to have some competition, and my mate provided just that. I couldn't have cared, as all I wanted to do was get a good mark and move on. What goes through the mind of a teenager at such times is not understood by anyone. Why would it be if they choose to keep it to themselves?

* * *

THE SCHOLARSHIP WAS AN external examination held at the end of primary school when students were generally aged thirteen or fourteen. It dominated Queensland education for ninety years from 1873 until 1962.

For much of that period, passing the examination was the only opportunity for most children to enter into the limited publicly funded secondary education. It was also the first external competitive examination for limited places in the early grammar schools, and later as a qualifying examination for the limited entrance placements to secondary schools. This was later improved to allow education for all after more secondary schools were built.

University places became academically elite, with limited courses, and the more difficult the course, the harder it was to get into. Places were therefore limited to subject choice and pass results in subjects suitable for a particular discipline.

This form of education, no matter which way you look at it, was one which discriminated by intelligence. But is there any other way to discover ability?

Most teenage children can do no wrong in their parents' eyes until they actually do. This can manifest itself in boasting and it can rub off in many ways upon the child. They sometimes think they are invincible and the most intelligent person on the planet. I have met many people like that.

After the scholarship results had been collated they were sent to the various schools. I remember hearing a distinctive tap on the door at the Taringa police house which was code that my friend Andrew was there. He had his scholarship results written on a piece of paper to compare with mine. It pains me to write this, but I had an overall result in the mid-nineties, which shocked everybody, including myself. He was defeated.

So one can see that education is a societal-determining issue, which had greater ramifications then than what we see today. Mind you, today, one might have to trip over foreign students on their way to getting a placement with the level of immigration making things difficult for Australian citizens.

In turn, demographics are subsequently a product of education and future employment, with those who are in special disciplines obviously more favoured than those engaged in environmental activities, depending on the governments of the day. The Great Barrier Reef has died several times in my lifetime. There were those pesky starfish in the 1960s, and now it is global warming causing bleaching and the left-wing United Nations fired up (excuse the pun) and saying it is doomed unless money is poured into rehabilitation.

So it pays to learn the periodic table at high school and continue with one's sums as they develop into algebra, precursors for physics and chemistry, indeed all the sciences. The arts were boring and those who chose that direction usually finished up as teachers with little experience.

Mr O'Shea phoned me at home and congratulated me on my results. 'I knew you could do it,' he said as he carefully chose his words; the other call would have been, 'Bad luck, what are you going to do? You did your best, ya de ya', and so on.

It was an unusual two-pronged call to receive as he raised the issue of that detention and asked me if I had told my father, and in reply, I said, 'No'. That I had taken the rap made him literally sigh on the phone with relief. This was a better result for him.

And that was the parting of our ways as I went forth to secondary school. But which one?

* * *

Towards the end of our state primary school years, we had a vocational guidance person and nurse come to interview us one by one. Thumbing through my report card notes, which were supposedly confidential, they decided what I most likely would become; whilst the nurse looked for my health status.

All were seconded to the Education Department. Sitting back in his chair with a cheap tie wrapped and twisted around his enlarged neck, wearing a white business shirt, this vocational guidance man finally sat back in the school library secretary's chair and stated it was clear to him that I would be an ideal candidate to join a bank, or, he firmly stated, that public service was an opportunity.

With a frown now appearing on his sweating forehead he said that while both required entrance examinations, he felt I was able with a bit of brushing up to pass one or the other. His justification was that I was good with sums, which he had noticed while flipping through my report cards. He then produced a Commonwealth Bank brochure, which he gave me with a smile, which offered a slight change to his bland demeanour.

This was the same bank which gave all state school students cheap tin CBA money boxes in grade five as a lure to create a CBA savings account. When the money box was full, the small change was better in the CBA than under your mattress. Clever, really, as you had to put the loose change somewhere.

Naturally, when the new account was opened at a post office or CBA branch, the smiling teller would offer another money box. This was advertised as a way of teaching youngsters to save for a better future. This was a time of grilled teller windows and no ATMs. The CBA was then government owned. It was privatised some years later with an IPO of shares. I managed to buy some at the issue price. My then accountant (who was a friend at the time) said at the Long Bar at Tattersalls Club, Brisbane, it was money for jam.

My friend at a large share trading firm once said of all banks that after brothels they are the most protected and profitable industry. Both had an insured and assured income. An assured investment is what one requires if lucky enough to buy shares. Remembering this a few years ago when visiting Pompeii's ruins in Italy, I saw this to be true where they had brothels for the most ancient of professions. Set in a streetscape of different sexual choices it brought a wry smile to my face. Anyone looking at me probably thought I was perverted. Either way, it is true of banks as they have a legislated monopoly. Bit like general practitioners, with a guaranteed income from the socialised Medicare rebate to the patient. As a pharmacist, I had a lot to do with GPs and have found that the vast majority have no idea of business affairs. Intelligently thick, one might say, but arrogant to the point of not asking advice from a professional accountant. Still, they have that guaranteed income, albeit with being on a nothing level in medicine as compared to specialists. These are the men and women for whom I have great admiration and respect. I also have great respect for the nursing profession.

* * *

APART FROM HAVING THE fever early on in Cairns my next brush with a caped nurse was at Taringa when we had a general medical examination. Asking me to cough as she held a stick spatula but I never found out the reason. Then there was the thermometer to take our temperatures, which was sterilised after each use in some antiseptic Dettol-like solution. Apparently I was OK.

This was around the time of the poliomyelitis pandemic – a debilitating neural disease now largely eradicated. Vaccinations of the dead virus are available in Australia, and boosters are recommended after ten years for polio patients in countries where it is still being discovered. There is no cure.

I remember well the fear of someone with no symptoms being in the community. Contaminated faeces was one way of contracting it, and I believe this may be one of the ways I had instilled in me an overreach in hygiene insofar as that is concerned.

When I was vaccinated, with three drops on the tongue, it was at a clinic held at the Baptist church, close by in Morrow Road. The church is still there in 2023. Many with disabilities from birth were thought to have had polio, because of limping along with the aid of a crutch, an indication of the aftermath of polio.

Such people were often ostracised for fear of being carriers of the virus. This was no different a situation to the plague, the Spanish flu in 1918, bird flu, and more recently, Covid. It is worth remembering that the Spanish flu was thought to have been kicked off from a chicken farmer in the USA contracting it from poultry and passing it on through the trenches of the First World War. It had nothing to do with Spain and killed more people than all the wars up to and including the Vietnam conflict.

So community health checks were under way at state schools, where a visiting nurse checked immunisation cards.

I believe I had a Mantoux test near my scholarship year. Fear of the needle was dissipated initially as the test consisted of several pin pricks together with some tuberculin virus. Any redlining would result in a check later (self-determined) and a review by the nurse when she called again. In 1907, Clemens von Piquet developed this skin test that put a small amount of tuberculin under the skin and measured the body's reaction. I definitely had a positive reaction.

There were mobile chest clinics around this time and also dental clinics in large caravans, somewhat like the blood collection units we see today.

After I wrote the above about community health, I talked to acquaintances I see each week and it was interesting that they recalled having the injections, but really did not know what they had had. One was going overseas (to Vietnam) and that of course tips the bucket towards the area of travel vaccinations. When I travelled, it was a requirement to have a smallpox vaccine which left a permanent scar after a reaction scab. Then one could travel with their vaccination certificate.

More recently, a Dr Ian Fraser, born in 1953, developed the Gardasil vaccine at the University of Queensland, and the rest is history in the prevention of cervical cancer. He is a Fellow of the Royal Society and takes his chair there with rightful reason. What a great step in preventative medicine.

Probably the most unassuming research scientist I knew was a physiology professor, Jack Pettigrew, the most engaging of men I have encountered. He specialised in stereopsis and had been spoken to for swinging an owl around at a UQ graduation ceremony. When he died in 2019, while in Tasmania, I felt he was walking to find what had happened to his already deceased brother, who was never found while walking along dangerous tracks in Tasmania.

It was a sad ending to a great engaging personality. He also was a Fellow of the Royal Society, who quipped to me one day that there were only so many chairs to fill at the Royal Society in London and they would have a lot of good scientists knocking on the door when he vacated the chair. He was bipolar and most of his research was tied to that.

When we last saw him at Toowong Village he was travelling to and from the Northern Territory studying cave bats and indigenous paintings. He believed the colours of those paintings were caused by nano microbial ingestion, secreting coloured infestation remains over thousands of years. His son was also a genius and dux of Brisbane Boys' College.

Dr David D ….was a BBC classmate who was very involved in the development of the CT scan imaging process and whose research resulted in a new outcome for diagnostics worldwide. He worked a lot with May and Baker, near Croydon, Surrey, in the United Kingdom.

He was hurt immeasurably by an incorrect blood test for

his wife, as a result of a mix up of names, or something to that effect. His father had been awarded the Military Cross in the Korean War.

The interpretation of the Mantoux test remains questionable in my mind and that of many others whom I know.

Somewhere along the line in the late sixties, and more than likely because of university requirements, I had a smallpox vaccine injection. The pussy pustule that resulted was a good take and my vaccinations card was duly stamped. I believe the vaccinations stopped in 1980.

Smallpox is an old disease, which also infected Indigenous people vying for trade opportunities along the Aboriginal trade routes throughout Australia. The Indonesian traders, coincidently, around the foundation of Australia, were thought to have infected the Aborigines to the extent that many died.

* * *

I WONDER IF IT was because my parents thought I would not win a place to a grammar school, or at worst, have to travel to a state high school, that led to my father charming his way in for an interview at BBC, to gain me entrance there.

The effect of the exam result was not a fait accompli as a low grade could lead to that bank teller's apprenticeship I had been recommended for, or into a trade of some description.

After the written examinations were over it was certainly not a time to discuss the paper with other students. It was a good idea to avoid the smug students. I vowed never to discuss examinations and pore over questions to see if one had the same result. You both could be wrong, which could raise false hopes and be very disheartening. I found those who engaged in this type of scrutiny were invariably small groups of females cleverly and quietly vying for one upmanship on their best friend. In time they happily resolved that one was the best student. So this discussion became a peer review, and all of them were happy as a result.

This happened all the time at university. Frankly it sickened me. After an examination I would get in the car or seek a lift and leave. Some of the guys would go for a cigarette and beer in George Street or at the Regatta Hotel. Despite considerable public objection, one notable George Street hotel, the Bellevue, was demolished in 1979 by the Country Party Government under then Premier Joh Bjelke-Petersen. And so what was once Brisbane's leading hotel was lost forever at the whim of an ill-informed government.

* * *

I suppose we had some sort of holiday up on the Sunshine Coast and Bribie Island during the Christmas vacation. No doubt we spent time at Caboolture and played some tennis in the hot steamy summer that had yet again befallen this subtropical domain. Mooloolaba had a cinema then near the surf club. That has since been replaced by shops or high-rise apartments.

After that usual break back in late 1950s, our thoughts turned towards secondary education. As a consequence of father's determination and focus on contacting reception at BBC I later had an interview with the headmaster, Mr Birtles. We were taken through the vestibule and past the tall fan cooling the room which housed this leader of the BBC community. The smell of the polished timber filled my nostrils as I sat with my father in his police uniform and probably also with mother gripping her long-handled purse.

After pleasantries we produced my scholarship results. Mr Birtles quickly flipped through, shifting somewhat in his studded leather chair. His narrow tie and a selection of punishment canes in the corner, together with his infliction of winking, were almost too much to behold for a fourteen-year-old. There was a lectern to one side with a large bible sitting on it. I wondered whether he read it between new student interviews. I learnt later it was there just for the holidays and on student days had a prominent place in the assembly hall, now the school chapel.

We were handed some sort of printed guidance, with the latest copy of the school publication, the *Portal* with its green cover. Most likely it would have been from the previous year (1957). My future headmaster pointed out that it would be worth reading as a guide to school life in the late 1950s and early 1960s. A bell sounded and the smell of cooked cabbage wafted up from some kitchen close by. Meals, yes, because near the main entrance and above was the boarders' area with dining and staff carefully chosen to oversee the older pubescent male boarders.

I must have somehow passed the test as my father presented a bank cheque for the first term fees, which were no doubt immense for a police officer in those days. We chatted as we left and walked up the steep entrance to BBC. I was completely awed by the size of the school and its beautiful architecture. As we walked out through the pillared entrance with the BBC emblem embossed into the cream-brick stucco, I glanced to the left and saw a grass tennis court and a grand home of one of the wealthy of the time. The cavity-brick, stuccoed building echoed the same appeal of architectural synthesis. I was to learn that upon the small rise of the school was the headmaster's house. Today the house holds an archival place the history of BBC. The tennis court has gone and has been consumed by a larger boarding house and dining hall. The school is much larger, having developed over time from a few hundred students and fifty or so boarders to boast a student population of 1100 pupils.

By now our walk had brought us to Kensington Terrace. I looked back over the buildings and noticed the creamy colour of more tennis courts down to the left, adjoining Moggill Road. To the right of the courts was a large green grass oval parallel to Moggill Road. Further over was the train line to Brisbane from Ipswich. Crows squawked in lovely sporadic gum trees, and tucked into the other road up from Moggill Road was another small building.

I resolved to find more out about that building when we visited the uniform shop for another added expense. The proud green-shirted BBC school uniform with grey flannelette hat and black shoes was the basic fare, unless you were a piper, in which case there was a kilt available. This linked the school to the Scottish Highlands and the Presbyterian faith, and the Wesleyan scribes of the Methodist faith. It was an anglicised

Presbyterian and Methodist Association (PMA) The familiar boater we see today around the school and Toowong Village was to return as the result of a vote by our year eleven students.

Together with the *Portal*, I was given a small stapled hymn booklet of school favourites which students had to learn. And there was the BBC school war cry, which was a must to know verbatim. I had to prove my confirmation had taken place so that the school knew I was of religious upbringing and intent. I still have the *Portal*s which were handed out at the end of each year. It was always nice to flick through them with another year over.

Photographs were taken of various sporting identities and each sport group was published in the *Portal* along with a report from the captain of that year's team. It was essentially a rugby-playing school in the finest tradition of the English public school. Cricket was also big, and the sound of bat to ball penetrated from the main oval up the hill on practice days and Saturday GPS fixtures. The rugby teams produced Australian national XV representatives (the Wallabies) and cricket less so, except for my friend, all-rounder John L….

Sport at GPS level was very competitive, but, with so much on offer even then, there was only so much you could do without having your studies affected. Rowing was big at BBC and in those days was held on the Brisbane River alongside Coronation Drive. BBC had a rowing shed next to Toowong Rowing Club. Other schools had rowing sheds dotted along the river. When I visited Henley on Thames many years later, the similarity was staggering. The quintessential event of the year was the Head of the River, which was navigationally very difficult because of tidal influence. The event later moved to a well-known dam. In our year twelve the Head of the River was won by BBC, and I remain friends with many of my former classmates today. They were all academically very successful.

BBC's postal address remains as Kensington Terrace, Toowong, and most of all that I glanced at on my enrolment interview day also remains. Especially, the war cry.

The privilege of attending an exclusive GPS school lay in the origins of UK money left and used to pay the relatively expensive fees of the time to send a police officer's son to BBC among those of greater means, not allowing for those who could afford to be boarders. Memories of BBC give cause for reflection as both my son and grandson attended (grandson currently). My daughter, Sara, also attended its sister school, Somerville House, which is now to be the place of Zoe, our only granddaughter.

I don't remember an awful lot of my four years at BBC. I made a few friends and for some inexplicable reason they included the inner circle of captain and vice-captain and others who were academically high achievers, combined with being very good at sport. No one ever talked about girlfriends at other schools, except for some passing comment when formals came around. There was always an undertow to relationships for each sport you played. There were the rugby followers, rowing followers and tennis, although not so much. I played tennis. Some were good at athletics, or thought they were and discovered this was not the case when comparing their results to those close to Olympic qualifying standards.

When I was there, in the postwar period, there was an

ordnance depot down by the main oval containing .303 rifles for instruction of the school cadets. In year eleven, everyone was encouraged to join the cadets, in an antiquated sign of the times. Some progressed to the rank of sergeant and others to a cadet under-officer. Some wore this with pride on the parade ground by the swimming pool. I did not join, as I was not allowed to by my parents. My mother suffered from anxiety at the thought of me going to the annual cadet camp held near the site of what is now the Wacol prison. I think some cadets got to actually fire a gun, for which I trusted all kept their heads down. Regular dad's army soldiers supervised the week-long camp held in the school holidays and into term time.

Those who did not join the army cadets or the Air Training Corp (ATC) were paraded at the special Wednesday morning assembly as conscientious objectors; this was to belittle us, no matter what our conviction. 'Fang', our name for headmaster Birtles, took pride of place at his lectern and nodded acceptance or otherwise that we were genuinely peace lovers. In the assembly hall (now the chapel) the prefects stood surrounding us as the school body sat in the longitudinal pews, subservient to all and sundry. Words were spoken by the school captain, who was usually a boarder whose parents had probably invited the headmaster to their large wheat or dairy farm for holidays.

With one's hymn book or prayer book resting on the front of the pew in church-like fashion, it seemed very hypocritical to demean someone in such a way. It pains me to talk about it today, such was the effect it had upon me. Conversely, it toughened me up and the only saviour I thought I might have was to stand tall and, where possible, defend my rights in a humorous way.

Some students were pleasant enough, others were little shits. My friend, 'AFP', from primary school was also at BBC and in the ATC. 'Makes a man out of you, character building' and similar crap was bandied about, which was tougher when even a teacher or two acted in the same way.

Lehmann (Herb) was a smoking lieutenant who proudly wore his army cadet uniform, which had nothing to do with the regular army. Mean-looking and with short cropped fair hair, he was the sports master, taught geography and had a nasty disposition that led him to snarl at anyone he did not like. He certainly did not like me and made that blatantly obvious. He did a good job of getting me singled out, with pathetic PE exercises after school.

You have to learn to swim, he would say, and towards the end of years eight and nine pulled me up the bell tower staircase, with its well-worn stone steps, and said that I should lose some weight before the start of the next term.

This was bullying from someone who enjoyed it, lest he succumb to his inner self who was, as far as I was concerned, a person of cowardice. He was always lurking in the background but as the years went on I just ignored him; so he picked on someone else. I was pleased for him when he took an extended break and everyone wished him well at assembly. I was ecstatic.

What got me through the bullying was a sense of humour and being given the nickname of Charlie. The name is still used and contemporaries and underlings continue uttering it with affection and conviction. It was a form of respect, and it was good and natural.

* * *

PETE LAWTON WHO HAD lost a kidney in action whilst flying Lancaster bombers in Europe, was my Mathematics 1 teacher. And as I recall, Mr McMurtrie was my Geography teacher.

Ivor was short, the other tall, and, unlike Herbie Lehmann, had actual serving colours from conflict. Iva was an average teacher but a good bloke who would sit us down on a Friday morning to study modern history, to the pleas of some students to hear what it was like to go to war. He went on to be head of International House at the University of Queensland, and he was awarded the Order of Australia (AO) as a member of the university's senate. I kept in touch with him for many years, when others did not. A tennis-playing friend of sorts knew him at International House, post his stint in the regular army infantry in Vietnam. J spoke ever so highly of Iva, Ivor as his saviour from the ravages of war. J completed his law degree. He had gone to TSS.

While for others joining the cadets or ATC was meant to be character building, for me not joining them helped develop a strength of character against adversity. The necessity for this was looming with fighting starting in Cambodia and North Vietnam. Several of my classmates were later to serve there, some in a voluntary capacity and others who were called up. That geopolitical problem exploded like the napalm used by the US in the jungles as I was ending my tertiary studies.

Up to this point I had faced various adversities, especially as my father had always been in his police uniform, and I was thus able to weather any reasonable storm at that time. This was the case when I rescued my father from a drunken wrestler outside Taringa police station. I heard my father calling and as I arrived I saw him pinned between two palings of the white picket fence facing Morrow Road. He was gasping for air when I set upon the normally fit wrestler who was relatively easy to put in a half-nelson arm lock to pull him off.

Blood trickled from dad's nose. As he wiped it off, he told me to bring the wrestler down the relatively steep concrete path at the side of the house and adjacent to the fish and chip shop. The police station office, a Department of Works addition, had slow-closing glass swing doors. Further on was the toilet and urinal, with its pungent smell. The other side of the police station office was a storage area which was our pretend lock up, as we grew up.

I assumed the glass doors were unlocked and so I kneed the now civilian-arrested individual through the doors. Unfortunately for him they were locked and his blood ran freely onto the floor's linoleum tiles as he fell, squirming in his own blood and screaming abuse with rage. He uttered profanities loud and clear, swearing I was going to be sued. That did not perturb me as he was the aggressor. The click of handcuffs behind his back did nothing to quell his angry resistance to arrest, not to mention an attempted murder charge if he didn't shut up.

It was up to my father what charge was laid as I slipped under the house to grab a bucket and mop to clean up the blood before the paddy wagon arrived.

There was always a bucket and mop there as the constable had to keep the place clean and tidy. A drunk's vomit on the floor from the day or night before was the last thing wanted in a ceiling-fan-cooled office where people came to complain about neighbours and pay fines. Some would be responding to various summonses. Even parents with wayward children would come to the local cop to seek advice. Often it was to plead a case for a teenager about to lose his licence after receiving too many fines. In a way, the local cop station doubled as an unofficial social service centre. No longer is that the case, as far as I know.

It was a time when only males were accepted into the Queensland Police Service. There was a shower under the house, where the mop and bucket were housed, and further on and under, it was possible to park two cars, which we did. Before a Mini Minor police car, there was a Harley Davison motor bike and sidecar, to the chagrin of an English police officer who had joined the QPS.

He was ever so confident with his rosy cheeks and fleshy build as he kick started the former US Military monster and set off up the road towards the strip shopping centre. He crashed when trying to U turn, finishing up the wall of Jack Shirin, the baker. Jack's shop, selling sticky cream buns and fresh sliced bread, was not open on Sundays, which was fortunate as the house to the right of the glass shopfront became the mounting platform after the constable turned left, instead of right.

Officers on night shift were discouraged by Sergeant Bert, my father, from playing games with the various handguns held and locked away on the premises. Some had been found, others handed in. There was an inventory. It included a Luger, which I admired. My father had a palm-sized Beretta which I occasionally fired at a target, especially on Guy Fawkes night. I fired it almost as often as I did the airgun at a target on a pine tree, down the back-yard. The range of the Beretta was disappointing.

One day, there was a rustle down the back where we had some chooks, which bordered on and above the railway line. I had my pump action airgun with me and a potato shot as a slug. Firing off the hip, I obviously hit something as there was an even greater kerfuffle in the tall bush.

The 303 boys brigade at school was rather envious when I occasionally mentioned all this, or 'AFP' had already done so. He had an impressive Blockbuster Canon, which raised the hills to Mt Cootha when ram loaded with gunpowder from firecrackers. This was impressive and my father was complicit by not answering the phone calls that came in after it was fired. The countdown was done over the phone to me and it was a magnificent noise spectacle! But I digress.

As for the drunken wrestler, I took my leave and he did lodge a complaint, but it was not internally sustained as the inspector from Roma Street HQ took routine action to quell any publicity.

* * *

HERBIE AT BBC WAS small fry as far as I was concerned. But he had the power of BBC behind him, which I had to respect.

Cowards need backing, as I had learnt a long time ago. He had the problem, not me, as far I was concerned.

In my senior years there was a chemistry teacher, named David Jays, who was from Sandgate and who I believe had a relative who had been a headmaster at the Shorncliffe state school that I had been loath to attend. David took an interest in my chemistry ability and I well remember engaging in a science research contest to determine the amount of citric acid in a lemon. These were precursor days to university.

I fully expected an A in chemistry, but that just did not occur with the external markers. That happens in examinations and there is nothing you can do about it. Re-marking was a possibility, but it was rare for a mark to be overturned. Make no mistake, it was very competitive to reach university, and to do it in pharmacy was even harder. There were limited entry level vacancies. To some extent I had my brother, who was working at Nundah under a pharmacist bearing the same name as eminent forensic scientist Bernie Spilsbury. So if I was influenced to do pharmacy, that was a definite reason, plus my general interest in chemistry and, to a lesser extent, in physics.

Our physics teacher, Mr Klieg, was notorious for asking the rowers for any mullet that landed in the boats at practice. He may also have taught me English in the senior year, which was bad luck yet again. His other claim to fame was to give 'AFP' six of the best for pulling a chair out from underneath someone during a class in the lower level physics laboratory near the main entrance. This was harshly offered, and a complaint from his father was received, but no action was taken.

A detention was sometimes offered as an alternative depending on the bad temperament or otherwise of the teacher. If they were having a bad day, it was your bad luck day as well. Fewer people took senior physics than senior chemistry. Detentions were a major issue for me as it was done on a Friday and there was no way of advising your parents why you would be late home. This later changed after I left. I did have the distinction of getting a Saturday morning detention, with the school dux-to-be for religious studies. 'Fang' thought we were dragging the chain, and we were singled out as an example for the others. Saturday at school in the headmaster's office was a novel experience.

Fortunately only one senior science subject was necessary for admission to the university pharmacy or general science course. People therefore rarely gravitated to other courses. What did happen was specialising in honours degrees and further on to masters, but rarely a PhD in pharmacy.

Senior physics and junior Latin were subjects I failed throughout the four years. There was no problem with the languages as only one was needed, which was French in my case.

I liked Latin, but the teacher, little Bill Williams, was old school nice with his white ermine-covered academic robes always a standout at assembly formal days. I sincerely believe Latin should be mandatory as a subject in all schools today.

THE SPORTING LIFE

The sporting teams were a real leveller, and with the encouragement of my parents, especially my father, I tried out for the first four in tennis. Getting into the team of four was one thing, but achieving a winning premiership was very difficult at GPS level.

John Loxton Murdoch, myself and Letherick North, a boarder, were successful in play-offs held after school down on the ant bed courts.

Reg Bellingham, a geography teacher from Wavell Heights, was in charge of tennis. He drifted in and out with his large fleshy appearance with button-down cardigan extending over his large waist. Nowadays BBC regularly produces premiership winners and the standard is far higher. At least it seemed that way when I watched BBC play BGS this year at BBC and end up the winners.

I was there in 2023 with my son and grandson shortly after I was in hospital for three weeks, at the Wesley, the same name as the house I was in at BBC. Fancutts have had a long association with BGS and the grandson was creamed in a good match against the BBC number one.

In my time, we always had a rotation of doubles and singles.

The event lasted all of Saturday, especially if we were playing away at TSS and TGS, which I did. TGS had boarders for ball boys and I recall the school insisted on including my dad for the meal of steamy steak and kidney pie in the boarders' dining hall. He downed it as anyone would do after an hour-plus drive from Brisbane to Toowoomba. I would have grabbed a lettuce salad and ham for lunch, something light as I was still to play later in the afternoon.

Then it was back to Brisbane in the EH Holden, with homework on the Sunday, a bit of sunburn to remember the matches, and formerly creamy-white Dunlop Slazenger sandshoes, now a very dirty sweaty sandy colour.

TGS was where I suffered cramps but kept on playing. We lost an important match we needed to win against CEGS when I faced off against a guy from Shorncliffe who was ranked at state level, as I believe I might have been from tournaments. John D defeated me. A chap named Brian Laver, and a couple of others of note, completed their premiership winning team. Ouch!

There was another Laver around at the time. He was a few years older with a lovely backhand and came to BBC when I was in year ten to play our then number one, Alastair R. Rod Laver was his name (cousin to Brian) and he conceded only two games. He used a Dunlop Maxply with natural gut strings, and we were amazed at how many racquets he had and how very good he was. He became one of the greatest players of all time and was nicknamed 'Rocket Rod'.

At the end of the year, after all the examinations had finished, we went back to BBC for a sports dinner for all those who had been awarded a 'full pocket' or 'half pocket' for sporting ability in the year now ending.

I had somehow received a full pocket and so did the others, except for North who got a half. Loxton had another year of school, so he was going to be back with another opportunity. Anyone with lines did not get to go, which was just the rules, and fair enough.

The late afternoon sun streamed through the stained-glass windows of the assembly hall as we tucked into the farewell and achievement dinner. Speeches were made and with the award in hand it was off to Pikes Menswear to have our pockets embroidered on to our blazers.

So that was that, and now I was a member of the Old Collegians' Association for 1962.

As I walked out of the school and through the tennis courts to Dad waiting with the EH under the Moreton Bay fig, I vowed that that was that for BBC as far as I was concerned.

Now, it hopefully was onwards and upwards to university studies.

Standing at the top of the stairs is Sister Denman, who was Sister-in-Charge at the time. The hospital closed in 1946, was cut into sections and moved.

Kilcoy Hospital circa 1945: (Qld Government Archives).
The Author was born 12th March 1945 at Kilcoy Hospital

Hambledon Sugar Mill (Web Sourced) Now Closed

*Hambledon State School, Class Photo: Edmonton Cairns North Qld
Author with Sleeveless Pullover on Up 3 Rows 5th in from left*

Figure Upper *Passport Holder (Can just see Aussie Coat of Arms)*
Lower Left *Rover 200TC (BXC 580G)* **Lower Right** *Post Card Home*

Left: Author (Rod) Brisbane Airport
Right: Postcard (Home)(no emails then)
Lower Right: Stonehenge Salisbury Plains UK

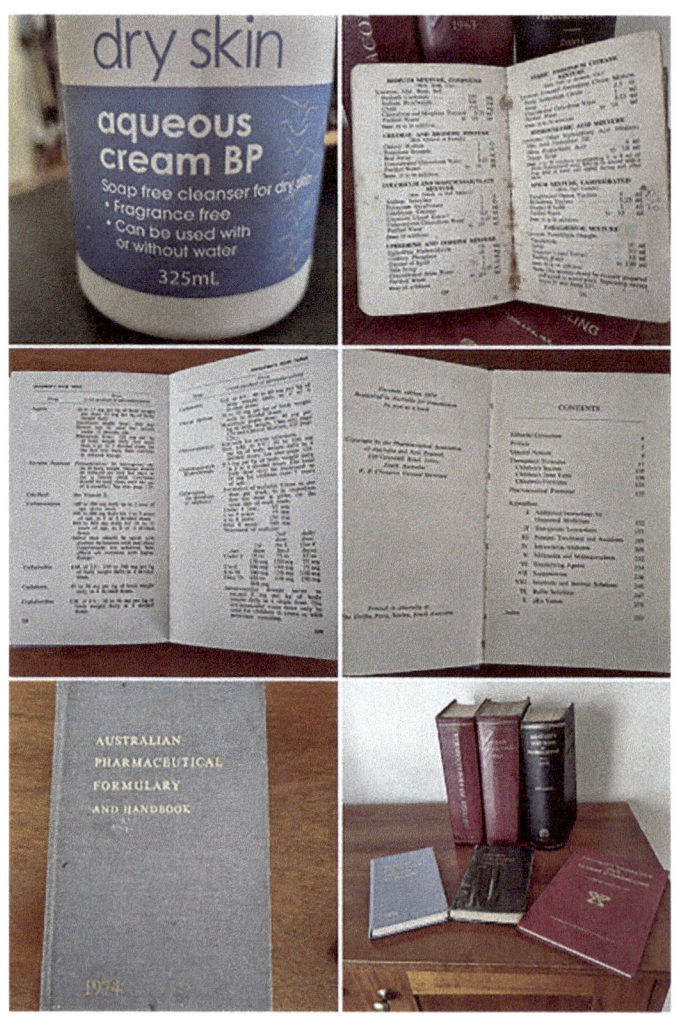

Top Left: *Over the Counter: (OTC) Aqueous Cream made to standards of the British Pharmacopoea (B.P.)* **Below Left**: *APF & Handbook 1974 (Formulary)* **Top Right**: *BNF Index* **Right Bottom**: *Six Pharmaceutical Books: the larger thin one is a guide to counselling.*

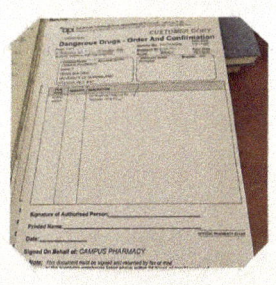

Left Middle: *Insert APF with home change of address (Just Registered in Qld 44 Morrow Road was The Taringa Police Station))*

Right Middle: *Dangerous Drugs Request Form.* **Bottom Left:** *Address written by Inspector as to where to dispose of Dangerous Drugs in Qld (in UK, DD's are known as "Controlled Drugs")*

Bottom Right: *This shows six Pharmaceutical Texts enlarging upon Top Centre Picture.*

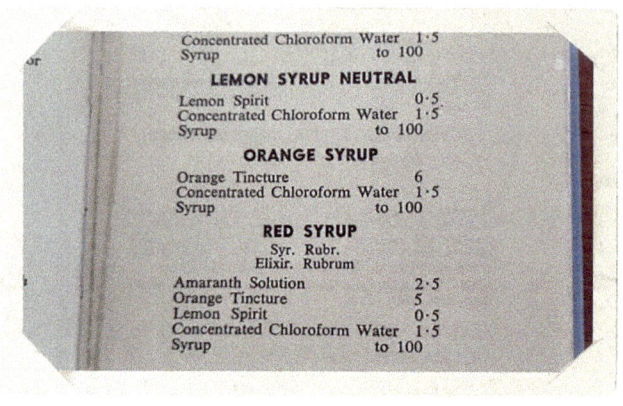

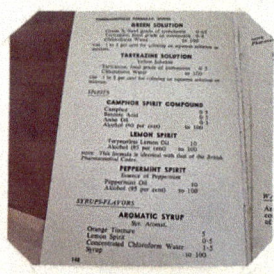
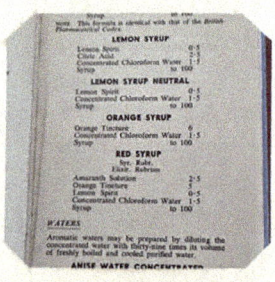
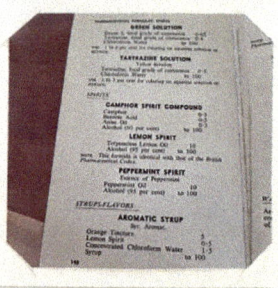
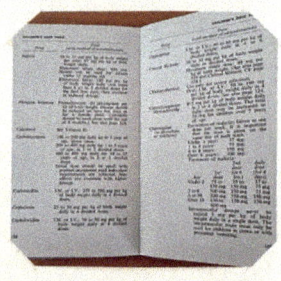

Syrup of Lemon

Syrup of Lemon would be used as flavouring, created from the Tincture of Lemon being as an Alcohol 90% infusion from lemon peel. This would then be added to pure Syrup, which would originally be made from Raw Sugar (specific, Weight to Volume [W/V]) [hence the need for heavy duty scales, rather than dispensing scales of more specific accuracy of measurement.} The sugar was dissolved with boiling water, which lasted quite a while because of its sheer density. Chloroform Water was used as a preservative in the correct amount to be bacteriostatic, but not in the Sugar Syrup. Over time this would be replaced, guided by the formulary, hence having its own expiry date which the Pharmacist marked as a preparation date on the Storage Bottle (Glass Jars with Glass stoppers). (Why Glass, well it was easier to clean, and in the old days a boy would be employed to clean the glass bottles. Some people would return their old Mixture Bottle when getting a repeat prescription. This could be Mist Gent Alk) for example.

Figure Chalk Powder, Lemon Oil, Rosemarin Ol.

℞

Galenicals' are products which are obtained by extraction from naturally occurring plant and earth products. This is shown above by the author. See Later English Roses notation.

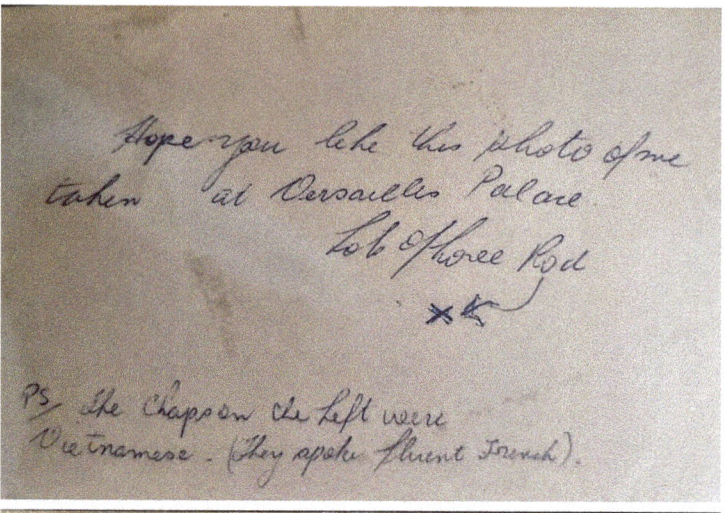

Picture: Post Card Top [V] with message to home: Post Card Bottom: Palace de Versailles France (Reverse Side of post card)

 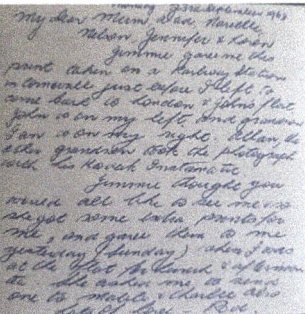

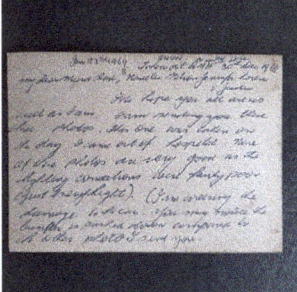 

Authors Photos
Top Left *With Viscount Simon II*: **Top Right and Bottom Left** *Post Cards*
Bottom *Right Rover BXC580G in Snow*

Collage Swinging Sixties

Carry on Nurse, Mikado, Baby Cham, Mary Quant

It is now not legally acceptable that sparkling wine grown in UK or Australia can be called "Champagne" Baby Cham would appear to be ahead of its time, with its return quite possible in one form of phonetically similar words.

Figure Cars of the Period.
Top Left *Ford Zephyr*
Right *1948 FX 6 Cylinder Holden Upper and* **Lower Right** *(Interior)*
Left *Holden 1964 Holden EH* **(source Just Cars)**

Family Medals: Left *Author (Vietnam) and below rising sun from slouch hat and tunic buttons.* **Father's** *Queen's Police Medal (rare)* **Grandfather's** *Boer War Medal with Bars*

Pharmacy Memorabilia (at home)

Figure: *Author's Photograph*

Chesham: UK Roses. Rose Water
Rose Petals in your bath, or on your bed in a fancy hotel? This ancient tradition has history back to Iran (Persia) discovered by a Pharmacist by name of Avicenna. During the Romanesque Period Roses were grown in the Middle East 79AD. **Rose Essential Oil** *(**Galenicals Essence of Rose Water**) is still used today by blending fragrances for men and women, which is quite an art form (Chanel19,Givenchy and home Alchemists et al.[Font water in Churches]*

Top *Bay Leaves.* **Mid Left** *Onion Johnny:* **Mid Right** *Branston Pickle*
Bottom *Barley Mow a typical English Pub*
(Popular with Gillian and Author).

Commonwealth Games 1982 Athletes Signatures (Selection)
Below (Some Stickpins)

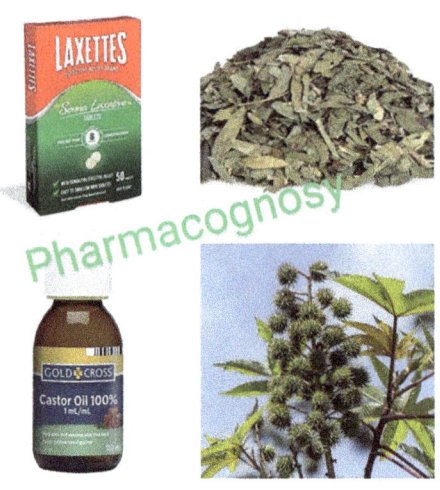

Figure *Pharmacognosy (生藥學...) Chinese Equivalent*
Senna: *top right* **Castor Oil**: *Bottom Left; Plant Bottom right.*

*Some Definitive Names for the Pharmacist
to learn or ultimately specialise in:-*

Pharmacognosy *(Drug/Knowledge) is the study of plants animals and microbes, which are found to have pharmaceutical application.*

***Pharmacology** *is the study of actions use and effects upon the body.*

Pharmaceutical Chemistry *is the chemical studies of drugs, a common drug Aspirin is illustrated below. It is not being shown in* **3D**.

$C_9H_8O_4 = CH_3COOC_6H_4COOH$ *(Aspirin or Acetylsalicylic Acid) has antipyretic anti-inflammatory, and anticoagulant properties. Commonly named as "blood thinner" If you add up the colours of the above, you see it is numerically equal in Carbon, Hydrogen and Oxygen. (So for Science at Secondary School the Periodic Table is fundamental.)*

Bio-Chemistry, **Pharmacokinetics, **Zoology**, **Botany** *are all chain linked to medicines of some form or another.*the study of the uptake of drugs and the effects by the body on that drug administration. It is a branch of* **Pharmacology.**

Senna flowers Arecaceae flower Bread Fruit on ground Cairns Botanical Gardens .October 2023

Figure: *Marriage Photos 4th April 1970 and Siblings Sara and Peter*

A married life begins.

C9H8O4 = CH3COOC6H4COOH

(Aspirin or Acetylsalicylic Acid) has antipyretic anti-inflammatory, and anticoagulant properties.

Commonly named as "blood thinner" If you add up the colours of the above, you see it is numerically equal in Carbon, Hydrogen and Oxygen. (So, for Science at Secondary School the Periodic Table is fundamental.)

ON TO UNIVERSITY

The waiting around for a place at university or a TAFE college seemed an eternity throughout December and January. On the other hand, the world was at one's feet, and one had to make the most of it.

It was only later that I realised how much respect I had from all my peers – those from different sporting codes and more privileged backgrounds. They had their own homes to go to and I was back to the police station at Taringa and 'AFP' at the top of the hill across the railway line, while I waited for the results.

The private schooling had a profound effect upon me and I was thankful for the opportunities it presented and for that relative in Portsmouth Dockyard (Brooks–Hunt) who had left money to my mother for education or whatever she saw fit. That, after all, was why we as a family had come down to Brisbane by circuitous means.

The majority of teachers at BBC were poor educators, and self-discipline was a must to achieve any outcome for a paying pupil. Now, going forward to university, this could be turned to an advantage. With a sudden independence of thought and attendance times, many who were admitted to university studies could not cope. There was no second chance for some degrees, particularly for pharmacy. I found this to be the case when informed I had been accepted into first year pharmacy at the University of Queensland. At that time there was only the one course, which was under the stewardship of a Professor Dare, from the United Kingdom.

In my brother's time a few years earlier, pharmacy had been at Queensland University of Technology (QUT). This was an apprenticeship course, which many regarded as a better training and a graduate result. It provided PhC recognition on completion of studies and practical work.

The newly developed pharmacy course under Professor Dare at the University of Queensland was within the faculty of science. The Dean of Science was Professor Plowman, a chemistry lecturer; chemistry was his research speciality with a special interest in azo dyes, which are used in the food and textile industries. It was humbling to meet people at the cutting edge of scientific discovery.

Three years of full-time study and passing all examinations would result in a B.Pharm degree. Before able to practise as a registered pharmacist, a further year was spent under a registered pharmacist who would report on the student's suitability after serving a number of hours at a lesser wage. Four years in total brought one to a point where they could work in retail pharmacy, or in government and hospital pharmacies.

Many in my year were to go into hospitals, which I thought was a good fit as no one taught a registered graduate how to manage a business, which took a certain degree of guts and natural ability.

I did my registration year at my brother's pharmacy in Stafford Road, Stafford, a suburb on Brisbane's north side, an area where Nelson has lived all his life. He has been extremely successful, but not necessarily the best of role models for me. However, I learnt a great deal by observation, knowing what will be will be. He was an aggressive tennis player, with a double-handed backhand which would go creaming straight at his opponent – an easy way to win a point.

But there was still the sibling rivalry mentioned earlier and this was now made worse by envy – often obvious in comments about my private education, not to mention my qualification as a Bachelor of Pharmacy. My argument that there was no other course seemed futile against his seemingly frustrated furore.

Yet he was loved by his customers, with many women bringing him cakes. I was serious and a deep thinker, and frankly, was not sure what he was like, except I worked my guts out during the registration year.

Counting tablets from a bulk supply was at the very least boring. Sudafed, Nembudeine and so on, Mysteclin-V in jars of 750 capsules (Parke-Davis) were packed on the Abbott Laboratories' counter where a specified length by breadth gave say twenty-five or multiples thereof. So the simple math with the Mysteclin-V was not to have any left over when you were counting the white-capped containers full of increments of twenty-five.

It was boring, but it was what a pharmacy did to dispense quickly to the patient. Nearby doctors' surgeries made it a ninety per cent probability that someone would come in after a long wait and demand a script to be dispensed as soon as possible.

Others enjoyed a chat and some would leave their script to be delivered.

* * *

NELSON ENJOYED DOING DELIVERIES, as they got him out of the restrictive environs of the pharmacy for a while.

For a time, when an order was placed with Drug Houses of Australia (DHA) it could be picked up down the road at a converted shop-cum-warehouse which they had established to provide a better service to pharmacies and therefore the patient. A few times I drove there in my Holden to pick up drugs for the pharmacy. Dangerous drugs were not stocked there because of the risk of crime or government regulations. I quickly learnt how much my professional life was being controlled in that respect. Nelson was quite into this and many thought he would have made a good lawyer. At the request of Professor Dare, he helped with lecturing final year pharmacy students in forensic pharmacy. He was very good at this as a combined result of experience and a natural affinity for all things legal.

It is important to understand that a pharmacist could be deregistered for not being on the premises while trading. There has to be a pharmacist always in attendance, and even leaving a shop assistant selling a scheduled packet of Codral cold tablets while you had gone for a necessary pee was a chargeable offence under Commonwealth and State rules. The Registration Board comprised pharmacists, lawyers, bureaucrats and Professor Dare, and most had no idea of retail pharmacy, but especially

Professor Dare, an academic.

Restrictions were imposed by government regulators, both federal and state. There were legal requirements within the state for trading hours, weights and measures, and recording dangerous drugs, which included liquids used in compounding, such as opium tincture. We made our own opiate squill linctus, which tasted better with a touch of syrupy squill honey. Linctuses did not generally require preservatives but, if they did, what to do was explained in the *Australian Pharmaceutical Formulary*. I still have my APF and also the *British National Formulary*, essentially recipe books for pharmacy. The moisturiser Aqueous Cream, which is no longer recommended, originated in that book, along with Sorbolene. Most commonly they were compounded/dispensed with one per cent sulphur and one per cent coal tar for acne preparations, psoriasis and suchlike. Sulphur has a surface tension which requires lowering with a surfactant such as tincture of quillaia so that it will mix with the hydrolic (bonded) creams. This is why we learnt organic chemistry, to understand the chemical or physical happenings when dispensing.

Nelson generally had the same lecturers as I did for pharmaceutical chemistry, and dispensing years two and three. The dispensing lecturer was on my back because he knew how good Nelson was when he taught him. I don't think he enjoyed the changes with the new course.

Nelson always had a stockpile of lost combs on the front seat of his car, as they invariably slid out when he sat down to drive. He was tough on himself and tough on the establishment, setting up the first day and night pharmacy when the government had restricted trading hours except for the friendly societies. They were a quirk of the policymakers. It was straight socialised medicine, under a co-operative health insurance system (friendly society). It was something I had to fear later where ownership was concerned.

If anyone thinks that walking into an all-hours pharmacy nowadays is the norm, they need to know it certainly would not exist without Nelson's determination and fighting years of government opposition in an example of the Country Party politics.

There was one other gem concerning standards control for retail pharmacy. This was the test script. Imagine being busy with a stack of scripts lined up and one of them is in fact, a test script. It always featured a mixture, inhalation, or something a bit tricky. It may have had four or five components which had to be compounded into a prescription safe for consumption. It may have contained phenobarbitone in an overdose, and, if not initialled by the prescribing doctor, would bring the test to an end without phoning the government doctor who had prostituted his duty of care by agreeing to write a stack of test scripts for the Department of Health. The health inspectors, with a diploma from TAFE, did the rest, encouraged by a supplied car and superannuation to boot. It was all big brother-like and could turn nasty if a severe mistake brought a pharmacist to the attention of the department in William Street.

Industrial inspectors were also visiting pharmacies every six months or so depending on where you were based. In country towns, their presence was hard to keep secret as they stood out like a single apple on top of an apple tree.

There was a pharmacy in Milton Road, Toowong, that received one of these visits on what must have been a hot day as the pharmacist was no longer being subservient. He was cautioned by the TAFE-trained industrial inspector for having only one glass stirring rod. The measures and everything else were correct with one plastic rod and two mortars of different sizes. There was a powder sieve of certain calibre, the benches were clean, the glass ointment slab was there; but shame, shame, you were doing so well but you should have two glass stirring rods, the inspector bellowed. His badly shaven face indicated a demand for perfection as this nasty little pharmacist had ignored his last visit. Shame, shame!

Unperturbed by this towering figure displaying influence and dominance, the pharmacist picked up the glass stirring rod and broke it in two. He put the two pieces back on the bench and raised his two fingers, or so the story goes. Needless to say he was picked on by these feral folk for months afterwards. Bullies, with their inferiority complex, are like that. They lack self-esteem, a bit like those politicians prominent in societies around the world.

The test script was also quite a performance, with it being divided into three parts. Say, for example, it was 200 mL of chloral hydrate mixture. That would be measured out on collection into three equal portions and labelled by the inspector. On one occasion, each portion was sealed with red wax. I kept one (defence), a second was for the pseudo patient (recipient), and the independent tester held the other. Had I done something to upset these people? No, heavily in debt I had just opened a pharmacy on the university campus, of which more is said later.

Who were these people? They were bloody self-important bureaucrats who got paid to do this. Archaic, is one word to describe it.

Miraculously, none of this seemed to apply in hospitals as far as I was able to ascertain from contemporaries working in that system. After all, they are run by the state government, albeit rather questionably according to almost daily media reports.

* * *

My apologies if I have been getting ahead of myself and the sequence of events may sometimes detour and stray from the main line.

Gradually, as you progress through life, you learn to dispose of problematic people. I spend every opportunity noting behavioural characteristics as these are dead giveaway as to background, health or social demography. So it is not surprising that pharmaceutical companies plot their drug output to align with socio-economic and demographic data. Let's take the example of type 2 diabetes, which is social in its demographic distribution. Near to Brisbane are places such as Logan, Ipswich, Wamuran and Mango Hill, which fall into this category.

Worldwide, obesity is the major factor where health problems exist. *You are what you eat* is very true, and the cost to health systems such as Medicare is subsequently profound. As a pharmacist, it is incumbent on me to maintain good health.

That is a useless endeavour without the constructive support of a partner because the rules state only a pharmacist can be in charge and a retail pharmacy simply cannot open without the pharmacist being there.

Add to this all the stress of day-to-day running of the business, intrinsic factors such as enforcing all the regulations and mostly the ever-present awareness that if a doctor makes a mistake and the pharmacist does not pick it up, it is the pharmacist who bears the brunt of legal, moral and ethical responsibility.

Little wonder that pharmacy is a highly respected profession as has been the case since the days of the early apothecary. The most important part of being a pharmacist is that the patient comes first, and that trust in one's advice is paramount to the best clinical care, as it goes beyond the actual drugs prescribed.

But instead of following this dogma, conscription and training for war came first …

THE CALL TO ARMS

Memories of my final days when I left BBC were of relief, and anxiety about the next step as life and its expectations were ahead. I had done the examinations; the results are now in the cabinet where I recently started to gather the memorabilia of life as a pharmacist.

Studying at the University of Queensland for a Bachelor of Pharmacy degree was satisfactorily achieved in three years with most of my cohort, apart from one, Eric Barton, who graduated also on 13 December 1965.

Both of us later realised that the Vietnam War and conscription to fight against communism were on our agenda as our birthday numbers tumbled from the lottery barrel of our future life, one that was chosen for us. Sadly Eric is no longer with us, but his wartime bride, Lyndel, still is and joins us for lunch with our long-time friends, Ross and Shirelle, who have strong connections to BBC.

The call to arms was kindly deferred so that those university graduates of all academic persuasions were allowed to become registered within the State Government of Queensland. The year passed quickly and I was fortunate to have completed my registration with my brother Nelson, a good mentor who was also a pharmacist who did much for the pharmacy world and received the MBE for his dedication. He is a deceptively reserved person with sincerity beyond question in this world. Narelle, his twin sister, became an acclaimed schoolteacher.

* * *

EVENTUALLY THE LETTER CAME telling me when to report to Enoggera Barracks in Brisbane along with other national service lottery 'winners', sent there at the whim of faceless politicians.

Medical tests were completed in a fashion like those of the Second World War or the Korean War. Then it was onward and upward to the Williamtown air force base and the scream of Sabre jets.

Upon arrival we were quickly given clothes with measurements not from any fashion house, including long johns and a great coat. Even now, some fifty years on, it sends shivers of unknown quantiles down my spine. Faked and real enthusiasm were abundant before we eventually settled into our beds that night with a side table and a spent cartridge of a .303 calibre bullet close by.

Over the following days and weeks tests were completed for officers' school and various relevant corps. Clever psychologists analysed decisions in what was a story of laughable professional neglect. And we were visited in a great hall by life insurance salesmen and told to fill out next of kin forms.

After a routine march in boots and all the kit, we had another medical test. I was summoned to be informed that red blood cells

(RBCs) were found in the random urine sample and taken by army ambulance to Liverpool army hospital in Sydney for further tests.

By now the attitude had changed to a one-to-one relationship, which was easier to handle. The army was looking after its own. Injured Australians from the Vietnam conflict were being flown home by Hercules Transport along with those on R&R and others who had actually retired from combat in far off jungles of despair in a third world country most had not heard about. Nor did they care. They were there to fight communism and go 'all the way with LBJ' – the US President Lyndon B Johnson following the John F Kennedy assassination.

No one back in Australia gave a cussed curse about the Vietnam War and its veterans were treated ever so badly. The situation has improved only slightly with the advent of the Department of Veterans' Affairs (DVA) with more recent conflicts.

The diagnosis of my condition by a young seconded general practitioner after giving me a cystoscopy was that the large mass was from vibrating polyps when in a dehydrated state while on route marches. After two weeks I was sent to 'the Heads', a nice staging post near the naval chapel for army people re-deploy and where I shared a room with an SAS guy.

I had a secondary haemorrhage which filled the toilet with blood. Don't touch, I was told, so that the staff sergeant could see for himself. It was a beautiful Saturday by the harbour in Sydney. A Macquarie Street specialist (DVA) asked if I wanted to stay in the army. I said no.

And that was that chapter over in the life of a registered pharmacist.

* * *

IT CAN ONLY BE said that the year of working and saving that followed felt strange, as in the military you do not have to think past your particular speciality. Meals are provided, with baked beans and bacon a feature of breakfasts.

Goal setting is talked about today as the way to overcome problems that emerge in our lives. I quickly found that opposition from various quarters did nothing to stymie my desire to buy, import and drive a car from the United Kingdom. I set my heart on a Rover four-door sports model 2000 TC, which in those days I could buy free of sales tax.

I ordered one in white and with hand stitched natural leather seats from the factory in the mid-north of England and sent a deposit. Now I needed to save £1300 for the airfare to the UK and balance for the car on arrival, where I would seek work as a pharmacist while also completing the purchase of the car. This meant working many hours at Nelson's pharmacy, day and night. I had previously bought a Holden from Leach Motors at Kedron/Grange. This bounced along thanks to the stability of the suspension priced into it by General Motors (GMH).

It was in the Holden that I had my first accident when driving along Milton Road and a car backed out into the main road. Even today, the possibility of that happening still exists in my mind, though not much is different along that road from earlier times except for the density of traffic. However, the original Milton Tennis Centre is long gone. No more grandstands or natural grass courts (the best in the world, Martina Navratilova told me) are to be found. Many epic Davis Cup matches were played there to packed stands especially between Australia and the USA. The Big Bill Edwards Stand was well known. Bill was also a pharmacist.

Banking was easier in those days, mostly because we had no alternative. It is similar now, but the use of actual currency in one's pocket is slowly diminishing. My hard work created a sum of money which was transferred to the National Westminster Bank in Piccadilly. I bought a one-way airfare with Qantas as I felt a return ticket was restrictive since I had no definite date.

This was an adventure of epic proportions. I remember stopping in India to refuel and ingesting copious amounts of orange juice while on the tarmac. I wonder where that steward is now – the one who told me to be aware of the distance between ground and aircraft. Those were also the days of smoking on aircraft in specified sections and younger, mostly female, attendants. We also stopped in Beirut to refuel and it was there that I went to a tower-like structure and bought a postcard and postage stamps from a box crawling with cockroaches. The day was one of balmy Mediterranean weather and I photographed at my peril some Russian MiG 21 fighter jets. It was my first time seeing guards with automatic weapons, although this did not faze me as we were called back to our plane now heavier with fuel.

As we flew over Switzerland I had my first look at glacial mountains and thought about returning there one day. Toblerone chocolate came to mind as well as then very expensive Lindt chocolate.

* * *

Though I was travelling alone, I was fortunate I had relatives to meet me at Heathrow Airport in London. My name was called as I reached the arrivals area and I was taken aside to meet Lord Simon, the chairman of the Port of London Authority (PLA). He was an impressive man and as we walked and talked I wondered what he thought of me from far away in the Antipodes. As a young person I was flabbergasted to be met outside Heathrow by the port authority's Rolls Royce, complete with chauffeur. No one took much notice as this was commonplace in a large developed country. London was a city in all respects, with Big Ben, bustling black cabs and red double-decker busses. Brisbane was an even smaller city than it relatively still is, little more than a country town, with only a few coffee shops and a Georgian post office with Georgian-style columns. But it did have cathedrals, with St John's being then known as the Church of England, as the change to Anglican was yet to occur.

The PLA had its headquarters close by the Tower of London and old merchant houses (ripe for Thames riverside developments years later) dealing in rice, tea, spices and tobacco. This was the East End of London, the domain of coloured immigrants, fewer than now, and where the infamous Kray brothers had their criminal kingdom. Car radios played music from a yet to be forever famous band called the Beatles.

The Rolls deposited me at the entrance to the PLA's head office and I was whisked away with luggage to the rooftop apartment, complete with bedrooms, richly decorated with wallpaper and plush carpet underfoot. I was directed to the lounge and later to one of several bedrooms, the like of which I had never experienced.

Sitting on the bed I felt the loneliness of being in another city, in another country I and many Australians longed to visit (Kangaroo Valley and the like). Did I feel isolated? Yes, to some extent, but I still had that Rover purchase to finalise and find work as a pharmacist.

I had visions of managing a pharmacy with 'digs' above, but those were few and far between. Those that were advertised in the *Pharmacy Journal* were all in unfamiliar places in London. I had registered as an agency pharmacist at a time when few worked in the National Health Service (NHS).

Eventually I accepted a position at Queen Mary's Hospital in Carshalton near Croydon in Surrey. It was close to Morden, and the Northern underground line. This meant leaving the extreme opulence and chef-prepared meals of the PLA's apartment that Viscount Simon said came with the chairman's position to accommodate visiting dignitaries, for trade and other seafaring matters. The first Viscount Simon was a Liberal and chancellor of the Exchequer during the time of Churchill. His oil portrait still remains in the Houses of Parliament in Westminster. I have seen it, but much later in life with the third Viscount Simon.

Twenty-eight pounds a week, after three months' of agency fees, was then a lot of money paid in the NHS system after a qualifying period; one usually ditched the agent and was obliged to have a contract of sorts with an NHS zone or group of hospitals, in my case centred in Croydon.

To be a student or registered nurse was really a labour of love considering the hours they worked. Board and lodging as low as GBP3.00 accrued fortnightly or so.

*　*　*

It was with some trepidation that I reported for my first day of work with Mrs MacDonald, the chief pharmacist at Queen Mary's Children's Hospital. We chatted about pay and hours, registering for income tax, the NHS and the like. Having private health insurance back home with the then Medical Benefits Fund (MBF), all this seemed so different. Such schemes were for the very wealthy in the UK at that time. Ironically the MBF was later bought out by BUPA, an English health fund.

I presented my registration certificate, which at that time was pretty much reciprocal with Australia. I had a one-year work visa, an Australian passport, RACQ international driver's licence for the car that was yet to arrive from Coventry due to strikes and other delays.

Mrs MacDonald was of Irish descent and spoke little of her private life as time went by, but that day she was brimming with the success of recruiting an Aussie, reputedly good workers, albeit they were usually there for merely a year.

Queen Mary's was built as the Southern Hospital in 1908. As local requirements changed, it was converted into a children's hospital and opened as the Children's Infirmary in 1909 and was renamed in 1915 after receiving a visit by Queen Mary. Six new blocks were completed in 1930.

It was heavily bombed during the Second World War and, after the war, it joined the NHS in 1948. It closed in 1993 after services were transferred to St Helier Hospital. Orchard Hill Hospital, providing long-stay mental health services to adults, remains on the site.

The 1960s were a time of change for nursing as the profession started to gain more independence and self-control, but it was a slow process. The sixties were the era of the mini skirt, but this certainly was not allowed with the measured, tailored student and nurse's outfits. Dresses had to be below the knee.

My wife, Gillian, and I visited the site in 2017. However, all we could see was a high school with an estate of new houses. We knew where the entrance had been and a few remaining strip shops still remained close by. I recalled buying Anadin tablets and postcards (now a rarity) in those shops, and long ago walking up the long driveway to the hospital entrance. Quite a hike for nurses, and those who had bicycles benefited a lot. The hospital was completely self-contained, with a nurses' dining hall and quarters and others for medicos and separate male nurse accommodation for which I was grateful.

Anadin is the only brand to offer a product range that includes ibuprofen, paracetamol and aspirin. This was the age before computers, when calculations of dosage were done by hand and math workings with at best the use of a Sharp calculator. And we had children's dosages to manage.

* * *

I REMEMBER 'MRS MAC' proudly introducing me to the hospital's dispensary area. On the way she pointed to a round jar with natural riverbed stones in the bottom. She asked if I had seen one of those before, and whether I might know what it had been used for. I looked long and hard and basically had no idea and, seeing my incapability, she said it was a leach jar. During the earlier days of apothecary medicine leaches were used to suck out blood and remove pus. It was a way of treating skin infections, such as ulcers and other *staphylococcus* infections.

This was a moment I would never forget. The dispensary, located in a wartime troop hangar, had been arranged with parallel benches similar to the much younger laboratories back at the University of Queensland. These benches had shelves beneath containing large bottles of bulk medicines and various additives for flavouring and preseserving usually over seven days on the wards to treat young children; such, were the contents of the bottles that they added to an odour of sweetness, which was yet sour and sweet. The stopper lids sometimes had remnants of a pouring with encrusted sugar around the lip. Well do I remember the bulk-size containers of medicines for children and adults, with a lower age limit of twelve. I was to dispense for much younger children and so reference books were necessary.

As I recall, there were age-to-dose tables in geometric order, which specified the dilution of Benylin (Benadryl in Australia and the USA), for example, from the twelve-year-old's dose to one for, say, a three-year-old. This type of dispensing was done daily from chits/charts brought by nurses on the many varied wards throughout the hospital.

The Queen Mary's Hospital spread over several acres in a pristine setting with separate roads for ambulances and porters. It had a mortician whom everyone knew about because when a child died he was known to wheel the dead infant in an old pram – a frightening disparity adding a touch of reality to the untimely ends of some sick children. You could hear the wheels squeak as he trundled his way to the morgue, located well away from the wards and close to the few garages that one could rent.

The dispensary also consisted of benches along the side with hopper windows, or those that latched with those adjustable holes similar to a leather belt. The permanent pharmacist, who lived close by in Sutton, was the diligent Miss Pearson, who appeared very naïve. This was the sixties, which saw the advent of sexual freedom along with the pill, the oral contraceptive for women. To be fair to Ms Pearson, she had only ever qualified and worked in dispensing for children the pill was hardly likely to be dispensed.

But there was one occasion when one of the resident female doctors ordered an O.C. (Oral Contraceptive) prescription for her own use. Supplies were in containers usually in 28-day packs per patient for use on the wards, and duly labelled by typewritten or handwritten warnings. They were also available for nurses. As bad luck or otherwise would have it, Ms Pearson took a month's supply of the pill and removed all the tablets, including the seven-day placebos, and meticulously placed all twenty-eight active and non-active tablets into a small amber pill container, labelling it 'one a day'.

Several of us watched in disbelief when the doctor, of whose attitude we were not all that fond, returned to collect her prescription. With an unfathomable expression upon her face she gave the container to 'Mrs Mac' who quietly and unobtrusively retrieved a strip from the original packet which she gave to the doctor, no payment from staff being required, and off she went having left the originals back in her London flat. Mrs Mac was outwardly a passive person and prone to blushing. I thought she would explode as we laughed uncontrollably.

* * *

AT THAT TIME QUEEN Mary's Hospital for Children (QMH) was a highly respected paediatric hospital in the UK rather than a general hospital like Guys and other large London hospitals. It was like a country town with wards from the wartime era. It specialised in research into spina bifida, a condition in which part of the neural tube fails to develop or close properly and thus leads to defects in the spinal cord and bones of the spine (vertebrae).

It was also a leader in shunt therapy. Many children with hydrocephalus were brought in from Middle Eastern countries for the best of treatment. Their parents were prepared to pay cash to jump the queue and receive priority treatment. The NHS did not work that way.

Many children were long-term patients suffering extreme conditions such as epilepsy and rarely from mundane issues such as the common cold unless infection occurred on the wards. Linoleum covered the floors which were kept meticulously clean, often by using phenol, an antibacterial disinfectant. However, it is caustic to the skin and inhalation is undesirable to say the least and so was eventually replaced by British-made Dettol, which was extensively used as an alcohol wipe during the Covid pandemic.

It was not uncommon to see a nurse or family together with a child patient in the hospital grounds. There was a seldom-used mini rail line which was renovated by local people in time for a spring fair held in the grounds beside the nursing staff club. The fair consisted of maypoles, coconut shies, lucky dips, face painting, helium balloons and a clown or two. A good time was had by all who attended, from patients, relatives and friends to local residents. Money raised went to the foundation trust.

A tour of the hospital grounds revealed remnants of a grass tennis court, and a special ward where a nurse worked who had won a contest to be crowned Miss UK Nurse.

Daffodils are commonplace in these cooler climates and were seen growing in profusion when they bloomed in spring along with daisies and jonquils. Making a daisy chain with child patients was a treat, and the smell of cut grass lingered long in the air. This springtime perfume contrasted greatly with the smell of phenol (which especially always tainted the atmosphere near the mortuary).

Popstar Cliff Richard lived not far from the hospital and was said to play badminton in a large hall on the grounds, although I never actually saw him.

Among the various dignitaries who visited the hospital during my time there was Princess Alexandra. The hospital named in her honour exists to this day in Brisbane.

I was fortunate to have a room and meals, but rarely ate much, though McVitie's chocolate orange biscuits, known as Jaffa cakes and which I was introduced to in the dispensary, were my favourite by far and are still available today. That was usually breakfast as I am not an early person. The dining hall was a little way away in a redbrick building close to the nurses' residences.

* * *

WHEN I LEFT THE army I was meant to have further cystoscopies to follow up any further development of the papillomas in my bladder. As I recall, I delayed it for twelve to eighteen months as I felt fine. I was not overweight, and even a bit on the thin side.

I guess the expectation of a new journey, the purchase of the ordered car, the meeting with relatives and a stint in a three-star London hotel while I finalised registration matters at Queen Mary's led me to putting it to the back of my mind for a while. When you are in your early twenties you feel invincible, regardless of any precarious situation.

While staying in the cheap hotel I met a lovely young lady from Kenya who was on holiday in London. She was happy to pay for her own gin and tonics while I had whatever was going, including beer on tap, which surprisingly included XXXX served as a lager.

Rather than gin and tonic she drank gin and bitter lemon. Later I gave her some boomerangs and other cheap memorabilia. But this did not entice her any further, even after several drinks. She had the sophistication and the desire to move on, and to shop in Oxford Street. I wonder where she is today.

Mrs Mac always had a jar of jelly beans or Smarties in her office and sometimes there were liquorice allsorts. She surreptitiously handed them out to those who popped in.

I early on determined this was her life; though married, she had no children. I assumed that the children of the hospital were her life for whom she had overall responsibility for care. Well, up to a point.

There were a couple of pharmacy registered technicians, one the longest employee, or as long at least as Ms Pearson. There is nothing worse than forgetting a person's name, but for now it is reflectively gone. She was an attractive person, tending to wear skirts like Mrs MacDonald. But she showed a femininity of closeness and friendliness towards me. This was demonstrated by drawing maps of locations to visit before, and particularly after, I was car mobile. Or she would produce the road maps of Britain. She was straight speaking, whereas Ms Pearson was prone to spinsterhood, by attitude and appearance.

I will call the pharmacy technician Ms H. Her only complaint was that she was paid less for doing the same job as a pharmacist, especially one who did not pull their fair share of work. This resentment bubbled beneath the surface like a cauldron of boiling water.

Like Mrs Mac, she was somewhat mothering towards me, but remained restrained with a conservative aloofness. Occasionally one of the women would bring in a cake when it was someone's birthday, and so it was a convivial place to work. One day, after I had been there a few weeks, I decided to have that follow-up cystoscopy. I approached Mrs Mac in her office and explained my situation along with a bit of medical history. I said it should only be a day off work and if I arranged it properly on a Friday before a weekend then all should be good. The dispensary was always short of staff, and I was genuinely concerned to not worsen that situation more than could be helped.

She was very helpful and contacted some of the hospital's specialists on my behalf. A few days later she said that without doubt I should go to St Mary's Hospital in Paddington, which I later learned was where Sir Alexander Fleming had discovered penicillin. I was given a referral to the kidney unit at St Mary's for the cystoscopy. This was a day-care procedure and if you could urinate afterwards you were sent on your way and would get the results later. I was given directions by Mrs Mac as to which trains and so on to catch. Even so, travelling up by public transport was difficult with the change of trains needed. Later, walking from one of those London trains, post discharge, was one of the most painful things I have done. Well do I remember walking up QMH's long driveway on a hot bitumen footpath with excruciating pain to the point of wishing to faint. This was the second time I felt very much alone. I eventually reached the cool brick interior of my hospital digs, and in a state of exhaustion sat down on my bed.

* * *

SOON AFTER THAT HARROWING event I received news that my Rover 2000TC was ready to be picked up from the Leyland factory in Solihull. They wanted me to sign registration and other papers and inspect it before taking delivery. One problem was getting there – and more were yet to come, as I was to discover. Having explained I was a pharmacist and needed to be at my workplace, it was decided to transport the car from Solihull to Sutton, which was close by.

Arguing over delivery costs went by the way and it eventually arrived at QMH. It was finally mine after all that time and effort, and there it was parked under a tree outside the dispensary, gathering bird poo. It smelt of leather in that way only new hand-stitched leather can. Please see photograph in the photo section.

However, when I came to insure it, all those I spoke to would not even entertain the idea. I was shattered. Lloyds of London had many members, one of whom I had been told to call should ever I need a chat. No second guessing that it was John Simon (Lord). He said he would make a few calls, which was the polite English way of saying 'this will be sorted'.

Within an hour or so a local Lloyds Insurance man called to ask for details and and said for around £300 he could insure it comprehensively. (The problems had been that I still had an international licence: the value of the car, my age and that it was ultimately for export as I had bought it tax free.) A sigh of relief came over me and I telephoned John to thank him. The car raised a few eyebrows around the hospital grounds. Parking was restricted at the admin building and the rest of the wards had limited visitor car parks. All parking was complex in the usual NHS large hospital way. I soon learned that, except for in the countryside, this confusing system of arrow directions and double and yellow lines was the same everywhere. For now, I decided to leave it outside my digs, and all seemed sweet for the time being. Everything was now organised thanks to a lot of assistance.

Something I have never forgotten is those who mean well, in the best and worst of times. They care, which is great, and it is what I must do. However, suffering stupidity was not my strongest point. It was the time of the Beatles and Simon and Garfunkel and I well remember John Denver's *I'm Leaving on a Jet Plane* as I looked out my window, gazing as far as I could see.

* * *

To this youngest son of a police officer at Taringa police station – which is still there in 2023 and 2024 and possibly up for sale – life was a financial struggle accompanied by a clear understanding of right and wrong.

I talked much with the hospital tech, not the one from Kent who was a Salvation Army devotee, and asked about places to drive to best see the delights of the English countryside. One day in the hospital dispensary, I missed a call from St Mary's Hospital and Mrs Mac later gave me a note giving details of whom to telephone. I knew this would be the results of the biopsy done some months earlier during the cystoscopy. When the Renal surgeon addressed me in a somewhat hushed tone stating he finally had the pathology results, I thought it was going to be renal cancer as a secondary to the papillomas found way back at Liverpool Army Hospital in Sydney.

I had returned to St Mary's after the first cystoscopy to provide a rather large container of urine after imbibing a large quantity of fluids in a cubicle near the corridor entrance. At the time it seemed to me they were still checking my RBCs as an ongoing follow-up.

To say the least, I was stunned when told I had renal tuberculosis as I had previously been vaccinated. It was a stunning shock to receive, especially when working in another country. I turned quite pale according to Mrs Mac later, who had surreptitiously tried to hear what was going on.

I learned later the pathology people had injected rabbits with my urine sample, to see their reaction. It takes around six weeks for them to become listless and have a loss of appetite if they test positive for TB, which in turn meant I had exactly that. The alert surgeon, who had done the second cystoscopy, had seen not a papilloma but a blister-like lesion in my bladder. I was in the right hospital at the right time as they were far more qualified than those back in Australia. He had seen this before with Africans but was astonished that as an Australian I had contracted not just a primary tuberculosis at some earlier stage in my life, but also this secondary infection. This was rare and still is today in Western civilisations.

There was a sense of relief and disbelief as I heard the pathology results on the phone. In those days most of the staff had been vaccinated and because I was from another NHS hospital, the reception was less formal than one would expect for a member of the general public. Because I had previously been on a surgical ward, I was re-admitted to the same ward. It consisted of a row of beds with curtains which a nurse could deftly swish together when privacy was required, such as when using a bedpan.

The nurse would later return, swish back the curtain and proceed to the bedpan area where everything was dutifully cleansed and the enamel pans hung up to dry. The white enamel on some had come away revealing black enamel underneath.

It was a men's surgical ward with a pressed metal ceiling from a bygone era. Several patients were bed-ridden, some because one leg, encased in plaster of Paris, was suspended by a pulley system after a motorbike accident or other fracturing experience. I was allocated a bed near the nurses' station. There was the occasional male nurse.

Mostly male porters scurried about. Robust female black West Indians performed the menial jobs of cleaning floors, oblivious to the circumstances of all around them.

Controversial politician Enoch Powell, famed for his 'Rivers of Blood' speech had been a vocal opponent of the indiscriminate migration of black, uneducated peoples from the West Indies. This had resulted in widespread protests, many of them violent and confrontational. At the same time, the West Indian cricket teams playing at the Oval, Edgbaston and other venues were welcomed in the English summer by the stiff upper lip members of such clubs and to a festive background of colourful outfits and bongo drums from the crowds of cricket enthusiasts.

It was a time when many males still wore bowler hats to work, carrying briefcase and newspapers as they travelled to work by the underground, bus and above ground railway from places such as Surbiton, Kingston, Sutton and Croydon. Paddington was the nearest underground station to the hospital I had been admitted to and the occasional rumble of trains was heard from deep beneath the building, especially at night if no other noises were around to drown it out.

I wonder if there was some truth in what Powell said; or is it just coincidence that illegal migration to Australia as well as the UK, France and others is still much discussed? The ward, with its rows of beds, would not be out of place as the setting for a scene in a war movie today. There were oxygen cylinders, and pressure cooker urns for sterilisation of instruments used on the ward, where glass syringes were slowly making way for what we see today under the brand name Terumo.

The beds were made of steel, adjustable upwards at the head and with washable foam mattresses. The majority of patients wore pyjamas with buttoned tops and a drawstring waist tie, plus an opening for a male to urinate. They were all in the same vertical stripe design and would not have looked out of place in a wartime concentration camp.

The creaks of the wire-sprung beds, which were routinely stripped for cleansing using a weak solution of Dettol or some chlorine compound, could be heard around the ward amongst the groans and chatting visitors bringing food, fruit and flowers. The many grapes always amazed me. There were and still are strict visiting hours, varied only on Sundays.

This was where I found myself changing from civilian clothes into these pyjamas (underpants necessary), as is the case when due to stay for three months, which I was not aware of at the time; but clearly the ones I had brought were not enough. I initially knew no one to assist me as all this confronted me. I had briefly met a staff nurse at QMH and there was also a somewhat gay guy in the digs where I lived who said he might help out. He said he had been to the famed Winchester public school.

The drugs of choice then were streptomycin (now rarely used, except in eye drops and fish tanks by vets) and para amino salicylic acid (PAS) served in a sachet form, now no longer seen much in the rice paper round containers of individual doses called cachets. It is a highly specific bacteriostatic agent active against *M. tuberculosis*. It acts in similar fashion to the sulphonamides – a competitive antagonism with PAS.

Isoniazid was also used and it is more than likely that I was given that as well. It all depended on the patient's tolerance to these drugs, and whether they destroyed the TB bacteria. Ongoing urine pathology was essential in selecting the drug used.

I suffered an anaphylactic response to the streptomycin. Adrenaline 1-1000 injection was ready beside my bed and a fan was switched on to cool me down. Eventually the heat in my cheeks reduced and breathing became easier. I had avoided a cardiac arrest. These days anyone allergic to animal bites or bee stings carries an epi pen with them to school or work to have it close by. Jan Simon (Viscount III) had one when we met in London.

One Sunday I had a visit from Lady Simon, Jan's mother, and everybody fussed around to make sure everything was tidy. She offered a cup of tea which I declined. She brought some chocolate almonds in a tin and said I was welcome to rest in their country house at St Just-in-Roseland in Cornwall.

As I recall, she may have only come once, as did Jane Gray, the paediatric nurse I was close to at Queen Mary's Children's Hospital. We remained as such until some of her envious friends put a few spokes into the relationship. Consequently, our relationship fell apart, though she did come all the way from London, where she was doing her general nursing course at Guys, to say hello in my digs on a few occasions. We had spent quite some time in the Rover parked in the laybys of rural Surrey, and talked a lot. But I felt she was firmly determined to be a farmer's wife, to someone I have never met.

She was from Rugby in Warwickshire and together we visited her house, where her mother was a firmly entrenched 'Brit'. I recall many times driving her back to Morden to the Underground's Northern line just before the last train at 10 pm. I took her to the West End to see *Oliver* and bought two *Oliver* souvenir magazines, which is a story in itself for later on.

* * *

Now back to St Mary's Paddington, where I was getting to know a few people as the weeks slowly went by. I remember feeling dirty as the clothes I wore were long overdue for a good wash; yet I stayed that way in the hope that someone would notice. Eventually a red-caped Australian nurse noticed that we needed some new pyjamas, and some laundry was quickly arranged. I felt much better after that.

I think the Canadian night nurse, who was staying near the ward in a nurse's room, had helped achieve this outcome. I visited her in her room and we sat and talked as she kept an eye out for anyone noticing I was missing. She eventually squared it with the deputy matron that I was a friend and she had been vaccinated against TB back in Canada.

So here I was on a surgical ward with an infectious disease and the thought of isolation in a fashionable country home never seem to enter into their NHS minds. However, it was in the back of mine and only placated by the suggestion I was different because of a secondary infection of TB as well as being employed in the NHS system.

This Canadian nurse, who was waiting for reciprocal registration, and I became friendly to the point we actually went out to London via the Underground and walked together in what was a surreal experience for a patient with TB on a surgical ward. She argued it was good for my morale. On days off, she took me out of that stuffy ward of death and I saw Piccadilly and the Christmas lights in Oxford Street and others being arranged in shop windows. We shared Canadian fruitcake and she knew London well. But although her kindness is remembered, by some strange quirk I never remembered her name.

Several of the male medical students learning on the wards as part of their medical studies decided that I was a guy who they would like to know, probably so as to meet this other Canadian girlfriend whom I will call Sally. They thought she was easy come easy go – frivolous would be my interpretation – in a lovely way. Each year, the medical school presented a pantomime and for my first Christmas in hospital I was invited to watch their rendition of *The Mikado*. I used a tunnel that ran from the main hospital to reach the medical school's theatre for their performance; and it was genuinely hilarious.

With Christmas fast approaching a very large Christmas tree decorated with lights and baubles was placed in the entrance foyer, where the smell of Brasso polish on the banisters could always be inhaled. Now it was joined by the lovely scent of the pine tree's needles. Nurses carrying candles gathered around to sing carols and the matron placed the Star of David at the top of the tree without falling of the ladder, a miracle in itself. The nurses then strolled through all the wards singing carols. And this was my first Christmas in London.

I suppose all hospitals have their traditions, such as the Wesley at Toowong when a chime sounds through the wards when a baby is born. And although I have been in hospital in New Zealand in 2022 at Dunedin Hospital, with Covid, close to Christmas, nothing matches my memories of this Christmas in hospital in London in the late 1960s. A large turkey, beautifully cooked, was wheeled into the surgical ward, complete with vegetable trimmings. With much jovial pomp and ceremony, the lead surgeon arrived dressed in his freshly starched white coat and expertly carved the turkey. Nurses delivered the plated servings with the all-important gravy over the white meat. Carol singers came to sing and a lone tear ran down my cheek.

It was cold outside and I gazed out in the hope of some snow falling. But it rarely does in London at that time of year. As I later discovered, a White Christmas is unusual.

* * *

BY NOW I WAS over the anaphylaxis and had been prescribed a

new pharmaceutical called cycloserine for drug resistance and fewer side effects. Capsules were prescribed to be taken daily over the next few weeks, and with good effect, as shown from the pathology tests.

This was one of the leading UTI hospitals, with significant outpatient clinics for venereal diseases, rampant among coloured people, who were predominantly receiving penicillin. The outpatients' department regularly received patients from bashings, stabbings and drug and alcohol excess, with police and ambos mingling among them. Its busiest time was during the weekend.

Occasionally on a Sunday night some of the residents and registrars, along with a few nurses, would clear a nearby theatre and have a party. Spirits and beer were produced in copious amounts and on at least a few occasions I was included. It was like a Sid James carry on comedy of the period, such as *Carry On Nurse*.

This is also the season when Scottish people's liking for haggis, black pudding, plenty of beer, and above all, Whisky, comes to the fore. So it was a few beds down from me was a terminally ill patient imbibing Brompton cocktails – a mixture of alcohol, morphine and cocaine given to control severe pain in the terminally ill, especially those dying of cancer and which I was later to dispense regularly in Poole General Hospital.

An intern arrived and produced from his lab coat pocket a half bottle of Johnny Walker which he had acquired by dubious means from the staff club bar. I joined the three of them and the Scottish gentleman was as happy as could be, laughing, telling stories and the like, as he consumed much of the bottle. Other patients stirred at the noise as this was around 11 pm.

He died early the next morning and all was quiet in that bed after that until another patient was admitted.

I learnt a lot from that experience.

* * *

Not long after that, I was allowed to be discharged and return to QMH at Carshalton Beeches, where I was to recuperate in the sick bay where I was worried about my car which had been garaged for the winter.

In the UK, space is at a premium and those with money who have always bought cars such as the Aston Martin house them in a garage but not necessarily close to where they live. I mused at how all those expensive cars being driven in the misty rain and slushy puddles remained so clean. Well, they simply could afford to have them cleaned; this age of old money afforded them the luxury of cleaning and drivers well before we did in the Antipodes. Today, self-storage for cars has evolved as a consequence and the purchase of garaging space, even in Australia, can be a good investment. Through sheer luck, I was able to house my car in one of four garages at QMH for sick children while I was in the London St Mary's hospital.

I ventured from the sick bay and my heart sank as I raised the creaky door to see the car was intact with flat tyres, which in those days had inner tubes as distinct from the tyres of today. To make it worse, the battery was flat, but the smell of that caged leather proved very comforting. Groundsmen and porters were obliging, and it was towed to the nearest petrol station, where everything was fixed. I can't recall claiming anything from Lloyd's, but no doubt I gave it my best shot regardless.

Having returned eventually to work and feeling much stronger, I began to use the car for outings. On one such occasion I had taken Jane Gray to Warwick and was hit in the boot at a roundabout on the motorway turnoff to Rugby. To be honest, the Ford Fiesta that hit me with its pointed front lights was not at fault. Jane had indicated this was the turn-off and I quickly changed gears to save braking. Giving way to the car on my right at the roundabout, with the noise of the motorway roaring above, was punctuated by the screaming of brakes on bitumen. Bearing down upon us was the Ford Fiesta. I quickly slipped the Rover into neutral and we finished across the road in the middle of the roundabout. Steam rose into the air from his vehicle on a foggy midland day. It was a write-off.

But there were good times in the car, not just the layby parking, and especially when the tennis was on at Wimbledon. It was a time when Rod Laver, Roy Emmerson, Maurice Guse, Ken Fletcher and many other Queenslanders had dominated the world rankings.

When I left for the UK, I took a Pharmacy Guild sticker which I had now placed on the Rover's windscreen, just above the registration sticker in a pocket-like replacement voucher. It was the pharmacy technician who encouraged me to go to see some tennis, explaining that if I went after work, being an Australian, which local enthusiasts would easily detect from my accent, they would give me their day pass ticket when they were leaving.

Full of confidence, with directions given (a mud map) I

arrived at a much smaller Wimbledon All English Tennis Club than exists today. As there was no parking in the park over the road, I drove up to the entrance only to be stopped by security. I pointed to the guild sticker, mumbled that I was from the Swiss Embassy, and they waved me in.

* * *

THERE WAS A MALE nurse in the same digs as me who, when I first met him, came across as rather animalistic towards females, laughing at taking away their virginity and waltzing off for another conquest and with no respect. This taught me a lot. Needless to say, the gay fellow, who let me down with a broken promise to do some basic washing and excuses upon excuses, had long gone. Thank goodness.

To another person I met I suggested we could fly to Paris for an Easter using our accrued days off. It turned out to be an eventful few days. We stayed at a lovely little hotel in the Latin Quarter. It was certainly not what you may be thinking as we both were as straight as an arrow.

The thing to do was visit the famous Moulin Rouge, with its bright spinning windmill and sparkling lights which came alive as night fell under a rising moon.

It was located on a strip that unbeknown to us was full of brothels. We went unknowingly into one venue which we thought might be cheaper than the Moulin Rouge with dancing girls who had not made it to the stage at its famous neighbour which was so steeped in artistic history. We ordered the cheapest thing we could find, which I recall was cheese and biscuits. A man speaking French approached us as we sat in the front row and offered us a free glass of champagne. We duly quaffed this down which he told us could be bought for about twenty francs a glass; or real French Champagne with trimmings could be had with the purchase of a bottle. I knew about spiked drinks even in those days, but my friend bought a bottle, which I worked out cost about £90, for drinking while watching the show.

Suddenly I felt the tickle of fingers on the back of my neck and in my hair. Two leotard-clad ladies of the night had appeared. They sat on our knees and offered for another bottle to be our guests for the rest of the night. I refused, as this was getting to be expensive. I asked them to leave. They immediately assailed us with a vile torrent of abuse in French and English. We were gay bastards, poofters and whatever other expletives one could imagine.

My friend quickly saw the wisdom of leaving, though when we got outside he realised his pocket had been picked and was without passport, money and the like. Between us we had just enough money to pay the hotel and eat French breadsticks (yum) with cheese and a light salad. He had also lost his airline ticket and we had had money stolen from our hotel. This was a disaster and we had no idea what to do. On the Sunday morning I phoned the Australian Embassy but got a recorded message, which was appalling.

My friend had more luck with the British Embassy. Despite the useless response from the Australian Embassy, they acknowledged my Aussie passport and they advanced money for the flight home, doing all the paperwork on a Sunday, no less, including managing to book flights from the embassy when flights on BA were packed.

We landed happily back at Heathrow with my passport stamped for another twelve months. A nice outcome, at a time it paid to be polite and drop a few names. I paid them back from my National Westminster account and the debt was duly removed.

* * *

I HAD LONG HELD AN ambition to go to visit the Lake District and Scotland, and I had a car very suitable to motorway driving to do just that.

Like most tourists, I was intrigued and attracted by the Lake District's reported beauty and even that long ago it was a very busy place to visit. All bed and breakfasts were booked out, but I figured with a warm jumper and coat I could find somewhere to sleep in the car.

As I didn't work on Saturdays, I had the weekend in which to drive up to the Lake District. What an amazing sight to behold. And it was just like the pictures on my old wooden lacquered school ruler. Whether the ruler was a hand-me-down, it matters not, as it was my favourite, looking after it as I went to school even with the steady advance of technology.

I have discovered that no matter where you go you always meet someone of Scottish descent, and often more Scottish than those living in Scotland. I had heard about the whisky trail in Scotland and found a brochure to guide me around it, buying miniatures as I went. I gave some to my future father-in-law a year later. I saved one or two in the most beautiful of bottles. Scotch does improve over time, so I wonder where they are now.

Many visitors to Scotland flock to Balmoral, one of the homes of King Charles and Queen Camilla, holders of the purse strings of a bygone era. People rush to see them as if they are rock stars in what has been a historically reported dysfunctional monarchy. I confess that I have done the same, as someone from the Antipodes.

But there is more to Scotland, such as its islands, complete with beetles and midges, something I was used to as the midges formed a cloud around the Rover.

With low cloud and swirling mists, winding roads between lush and not so lush pastures, horrible yellow-flowered gorse that tears your skin, Scotland is one of the most beautiful places to drive. With black-nosed sheep, and their traditional herders, it seems almost Biblical at times. Probably the most beautiful island is the Isle of Skye, but when I visited, it seemed murky with cloud almost enveloping everywhere.

Although frequently described as traditional, *The Skye Boat Song* was written and published by Harold Boulton in the 19th century with a melody by Annie MacLeod that was based on a traditional tune. It recalls the journey of Prince Charles Edward Stuart (Bonnie Prince Charlie) from Benbecula to the Isle of Skye as he evaded capture by government troops after his defeat at the Battle of Culloden in 1746.

Former Beatle Paul McCartney and Denny Laine wrote *Mull of Kintyre* about the island, which McCartney bought in 1966.

The song, performed by his band Wings, topped the charts.

* * *

ON A JOURNEY TO Scotland with a Ugandan pharmacist colleague we stopped somewhere where many of the residents were legitimate migrants. My companion was from a different background and culture to that of the other QMH who was proud of his female conquests.

His family, who lived in Leeds, welcomed us with immense pleasure when we arrived. I recall, drops of fabric partitioned rooms into separate parts. They were proud of their son and showed no animosity to this Aussie white fellow. It was a time when apartheid still existed in South Africa, and Uganda was close to becoming a dictatorship as a new republican constitution abolished the kingdoms altogether. Uganda was divided into four districts and ruled by martial law, a forerunner of the military domination the country would experience after 1971 under the brutal Idi Amin.

My welcome in Leeds was a surprise, given that Australia was still well known for its white Australia policy, which was ended by the Labor Whitlam Government in 1973.

On arrival, we were given a hot curry meal with rice which I awkwardly devoured with my fingers, water and a spoon. After presents were exchanged, we then went to stay the night with his Leeds University mates in a rental university apartment. It was bohemian to say the least and my Ugandan colleague advised me to make sure I completely zipped up the sleeping bag because of the possibility of bed bugs and lice biting and infiltrating the covers we had for the journey. A quick beer and decline to smoke cigarettes, no matter what the filling was, in this darkened noisy room, were in my thoughts when we left early the next morning. I wonder where those Psychology 101 students are today.

So we continued due north with me driving, stopping for fuel only a couple of times and thinking we would do a B&B somewhere in Scotland which we found appealing.

We tried several and although they displayed vacancy signs, my travelling friend returned each time to the car saying in his black husky voice that they were full up.

While we were both amazed, we did have more than an inkling that because he was black, they expected him to be too unclean to stay in their house.

As it was getting towards 11 pm, we came upon a beautiful stone cottage by a babbling brook, which, with its purity, doubtless fed many distilleries. It was drinkable fresh water from some glacial melting. But we still had to approach the Scottish landlord to stay in a B&B for a few days.

So with a smile to my friend, I got out of the car. A curtain was pulled back as I approached the curious owners. The northern lights were beginning to darken and I felt the inspiration of Robert Burns, and his poetry, from nearby Dumfries.

I noticed a sign of satisfaction come across the host's faces as they recognised the make of my car. I was welcomed, exchanged cash and a traveller's cheque, and said my friend would bring in our cases. In the fading light, their faces took a surprised fidgeting glancing look when they saw he was black. They probably thought we were gay, but black, that was the living end. But a contract to stay had to be met and they turned out to be very welcoming when they realised we were professional pharmacists.

So we finally had a base camp from which we were set to explore.

My friend had surreptitiously packed a shotgun and cartridges in the boot of the car and I was a little uncomfortable whether it would be safe if we were in a road accident or, God forbid, should we ever use it. But he reminded me that I had said I had always wanted to go grouse shooting. Unfortunately, in our naivety we failed to check that grouse shooting occurs from mid-August to early December – and we had missed that.

Not to be outdone we visited the famed St Andrew's golf links with the wind blowing a gale. But the lovely club was very toffy nosed; it was members only and no associate day members. So we walked across the deserted links to the beach amid the howling wind, complete with shotgun and a few cartridges. We argued that no one would see or hear us above the howling winds, while the toffs sipped their whiskies in the clubhouse. We learned that gorse is prickly and soon lost interest in looking for grouse.

Instead, there were screeching seagulls which provided excellent target practice until we ran out of shells. Years later my wife and I visited Leith, the old port of Edinburgh, where we were shown where golf actually began.

Scotland is indeed a beautiful place to visit.

* * *

THE SECOND TIME I experienced racism firsthand was on our honeymoon when we docked at Cape Town aboard the liner *Fairsky*. The Italian crew begged us to stay on board in their gesticulating emotional way, but the ship's doctor was outgoing and with some collective urging and sense of security, we left the ship at about dusk.

We were aware the docks were dangerous places where lower class blacks with TB and VD congregated. The smell of vomit tainted the air, as black South Africans disadvantaged by apartheid did the best they could among a white population that looked down upon them.

The thought of a cold beer on tap lured us towards the lights of a dockside pub. I was told they would be jailed or flogged if they served white people and we faced the likelihood of jailing as well. We ignored that and the GP and I gave them a handsome tip, which they truly deserved.

The third time I experienced racism was when I was parking my white Mercedes C 250 near the Olympic pool at the University of Queensland. This came from an olive-skinned female. On 7 September 2017, I wrote to the university's legal service:

> When visiting the University of Queensland St Lucia campus yesterday and in the process of rightfully parking, I received deliberate and unprovoked racial vilification. This was premeditated and happened at the time of paying. To be told that I supported white supremacy and "I hope you have a heart attack" was very confronting and very

inappropriate. To do that on a university campus towards a stranger shows even more contemptuous behaviour; and then just to simply walk away.

Nothing came of my complaint, though I still have the records years later that might help identify the perpetrator. The university checked her car registration but would not reveal the owner nor provide ownership details. They had kicked the can down the road.

As recently as 14 October 2023, Australia held a referendum on the Indigenous Voice to Parliament. It failed completely.

It is so easy to use the racist card when some people feel it is to their advantage. Politicians are no exceptions, nor large corporations.

But the people of Scotland really knew no better. They were still at the stage of naivety, where the dominant case of extinction by race was very much still the Holocaust. Indeed, there is a warring situation as I write, between Hamas and Israel.

Where racism is concerned, one wise person once said, 'It is not racist to talk about racism'.

* * *

THE RETURN DRIVE TO London was a memorable experience. With the bright night sky, scant fog and good roads we made excellent time to Yorkshire where I dropped off my passenger in his home city of Leeds. I do not recall hearing from him again.

I knew not to drive when tired and could hear the rattle of the whisky miniatures as I travelled along A roads, and for a while along B roads. It was not unusual on motorways to hit 100 mph, which when converted is 160 kph, and to be passed in the outside lane by Ferraris, Aston Martins and the occasional Porsche, even when driving at the permitted maximum. On wet roads the passing vehicles shot up a muddy spray so that wipers and cleaners were very much a necessity. It was the first time I experienced the flashing of headlights to indicate such situations as overtaking, allowing merging from a slip road and especially warning of a police radar trap ahead. This was in the days when the police still sat at a radar box beside the road to clock your speed.

There were plenty of roadside laybys with cafes which were perfect for breaking a journey – a stop for a cup of English breakfast tea and, invariably, bacon and eggs and Heinz baked beans. During the late sixties there were smoking areas where people huddled discussing who knows what. As you tucked into a full English breakfast, or the soup of the day such as pea and ham, minestrone or whatever was going, the noise of screaming cars in both directions punctuated the otherwise murky air.

Fatigue must never be ignored, especially when driving on your own. I was cranky from tiredness, coupled with nerves at the thought of driving on the North Circular and avoiding central London by using the M25, which is also the access to Heathrow airport and one of the busiest roads in the world. Exiting at the right spot would take me into Surrey and thence to Sutton with Carshalton not far away.

I eventually found a B road with a widened stretch which enabled a farmer to come in and out with his tractor. This seemed the perfect place to sleep in the car overnight. I had enough petrol to start the car and use the heater system to warm the car up. I had water and a packet of English digestive biscuits and Marmite, and that was dinner sorted.

After parking, I noticed a stile close by which I found useful to cross the fence and access an old oak tree and enjoy a much-needed pee. Stiles are very useful in the UK for walkers trekking along designated walking paths.

I fell asleep and woke with fogged-up windows to the sound of a tapping on the slightly open window. A police officer wanted to know what I was doing there. Put simply, I said I was sleeping, which produced a grunt or sniff of some sort. He inspected my international driver's licence, which raised some sort of disbelief in his mind. He had stopped his patrol car on the crunchy gravelly verge ahead of mine, probably thinking he had found a pair of lovers shacked up, or that mine was a stolen car. Seemingly satisfied after using his long-handled torch to good effect, he left me in the wilderness to finish my sleep.

The troubled sleep that followed brought me to the decision that as it was now early Sunday morning with about forty minutes to go to the outskirts of London, I would get an early start and avoid the traffic, still heavy but nothing like on working days.

I somehow missed my turning at the flyover and found myself driving directly across the River Thames via Westminster Bridge and, eventually, perplexed and somewhat fearful, I pulled up beside a policeman somewhere near Piccadilly Circus. With window down and me stretched out across the passenger seat, I asked the best way to exit London and find the road to Sutton. To my surprise, he ignored my requests and kept on walking. I later found out this was probably because gangland mobsters used similar techniques to distract police on the beat.

I drove on and was relieved to notice places that were reasonably familiar. It must have been Putney Bridge that I crossed and I then headed south, following signs to Richmond and Hampton Court, its brick wall parallel to me as I drove.

I followed the roundabout signs to Sutton and took a deep breath as I reached the QMH entrance. I parked the car in the lock-up garage down by the children's morgue and grabbed a couple of Anadin. The nurses were coming out of the dining hall as I walked in to grab some porridge, or whatever was going.

I was due back at work a few hours later and made it in the nick of time, albeit somewhat exhausted as I was still not as strong as I would normally be from the now treated TB.

They were all there and I gave a vial of perfume to Mrs MacDonald who blushed with acceptance and some Toblerone chocolates for the general staff. By now, another pharmacist had joined the group. This was Fergus, a New Zealander. I felt he was light on personality, but at least we could go for a drink in the staff club by the tennis court.

* * *

As TIME WENT BY I played some tennis on that grass court with someone who heard from the noticeboard that I was interested.

This led to matches against other clubs. I used the lovely Dunlop Volley racquet, made famous by Rod Laver.

One of our mixed team was reputedly an English county player and another was a physiotherapist. They were the two I remember most. Somewhere there is a tennis group photo, which I am yet to rediscover.

Tennis has always been my great love and on Saturday afternoons during summer we played at various places. One interesting venue was a nearby rehabilitation hospital for RAF personnel. They were 'right proper' and very polite. We remained friends for a while, with the Officers' Club being an amazing place to have a beer on tap. Most were RAF doctors, physiotherapists, occupational therapists and the like. I made sure I was on my polite side, though I did pull them up on a few tennis points, and also some military ones, including their lack of knowledge of the Australian commitment in Vietnam. They were absolutely well mannered but were fiercely competitive when it came to playing, to the point where line calls could be somewhat dubious! They were keen to win the premiership, which we actually won and received a trophy which I still have to track down.

In contrast, I also played at a prison compound for mental patients, where the echo of the balls resounding off the grey brick walls helped my timing. This surface was bitumen.

* * *

WE HAD A STAFF club at QMH which opened at irregular hours but was a good place to gather both in winter and in the long twilights of summer. It had the usual manual soccer game board, and there also may have been a dartboard, to relax, while drinking the limited beers, including lager, which was a new terminology to me.

This was the sixties when champagne was only for the wealthy. My first introduction to alcoholic beverages had been in the West Country area of England where scrumpy, made from fermented apples, was a popular drink. It is also quite alcoholic and before I knew it nearly sent me reeling.

But the alcoholic drink of the moment, and relatively cheap, was a product unique to England called Babycham. Given various crude labels, one of which was 'the leg opener', it is made from fermented pears and often shared with two Babycham glasses and sipped as the bubbles rose. I disliked it.

As nurses were paid very little, they went to the club and then often would share a drink. It was probably the chirp of a robin that I heard in the trees outside the club when I pulled up a chair to join a group of nurses who had the following day or so off. They might have been doing block exams, but the chance to have a chat with females was more on my mind. The female species is without doubt very difficult to understand, as most men, married or single, will often attest to.

Coming from Australia, I was bombarded by questions. In the UK they knew about kangaroos, boomerangs and the great size of Australia but that was mostly it. However, many envied the open spaces and beaches, as they still do today

We had barbecues and at that time they did not. A group of girls enjoying themselves at a table with wicker-backed chairs said they were happy for me to join them and it was with racing heart and mumbling awkwardness that I started a conversation. This routine developed over a few weeks usually with the same group of student nurses. One was Linda Baird and another was Gillian Brooks, who I recall going outside now and then to have a cigarette.

Gradually I gained confidence even to the point of one evening discussing sex before marriage. The girls shifted forward in their seats, Babycham glasses in their hands, waiting to hear what I had to say about the pill, the age of enlightenment and sexual freedom, but with the compunction to go for it hell for leather.

Remember, this was a time of man walking on the moon, the Cuban crisis, the Cold War, and Russia's invasion of what was then Czechoslovakia. But when one is young, one gets caught up in one's own moment and invincibility becomes the order of the day.

Very quickly, I had a response that tested my argument of retaining virginity before marriage. At that time English girls were far more sophisticated and mature than Australian ones, though with a dominating mother and a police officer father I had no experience to test that. In Australia at that time, it was very much boy meets girl with heads down while studying, some at high school, others at university. In my final year at the University of Queensland, I had been friendly with a girl whom I will call Miss UQ. We sat together over lunch down at the sheds on campus and enjoyed each other's company.

My favourite subject was pharmacognosy with the late Dr Griffin from the English Midlands as my lecturer, along with seventy or so other students in our year. All I knew was that this stunningly attractive student I sat next to had been Miss University at UQ. Feminists were developing small agitating groups, with some that chained themselves to the footrail of the Regatta Hotel, opposite the Brisbane River and the Toowong ferry. Jeans were banned at university, so girls wore skirts, some with stockings, and covered themselves with white lab coats.

That's a good pick-up line, I thought when seeming to be discussing sex and virginity, whereas I was actually discussing, on reflection, my own shortcomings. The girl at the club who I had met at times on the wards was the one called Gillian. She had a lovely smile.

This was not long after a friendship with a girl called Jean had ebbed and was not to be renewed.

Gillian and I grew closer together and my discussion on sex before marriage began to bite me on the bum as she reminded me when I tried it on. However, unlike Jean, she had no qualms about coming to my room nor was she bothered by authorities that said not to do so, in a convent sort of way.

Then, one day she was unable to see me, as when she could afford it, she would travel by train to Bournemouth, a resort on the south coast where her parents lived. Her sister Angela, a devotee of Billy Graham, the religious messiah, studied radiography in London while lodging in communal Baptist digs.

It was on these occasions that I realised I missed Gillian's smiling face, dare-to-do attitude and easy company upon which I was starting to rely.

I started to ask her about Bournemouth and found out

that it was in Hampshire, whereas in reality she lived in the neighbouring resort of Poole but officially in the county of Dorset. This stoked my curiosity – this was Thomas Hardy country and the home of the Tolpuddle Martyrs, where the trade union movement started when they were deported to Australia. How many in the ALP would know this apart from the odd immigrant shop steward who has come to Australia?

On a few occasions after work I drove down to Brighton, also on the south coast. Brighton was a disappointment, even though it had some Indian decorated palace, but there was no sand, just pebbles large enough to twist your ankle! But there was also the scent of the salty sea and, across the English Channel, lay France. I then realised that instead of her having to endure an hour or so on a slow train, I could take Gillian to her home in Dorset.

Her face lit up with that lovely smile as she said yes to giving her a lift when she had time off. This would be a couple of weeks away on a weekend starting with the Friday.

I had just taken time to visit physiotherapist Alice for some checking of muscles and we had a conversation which reminded me of acquiring my UK driving licence. I remembered that while at QMH I had not explained how I came to get my driving licence while in the UK – something that my future mother-in-law, Monica, kept renewing for me for countless years.

The nearest licence issuing point was in either Croydon or Sutton, perhaps a smaller office at Carshalton. When I pulled up outside there was a chauffeur standing as only they can when without a car. Inside I was met by an instructor who was going to test me on the basis of my existing two licences – a far cry from rocking up to Caboolture police station courtesy of my father and Uncle Jesse Hunt, when I got my first licence without a test.

The smell of carbon paper and the noise of typing and chatter, punctuated by critical comments, filled the air that Saturday in Croydon. Getting back into the car, I suffered the usual comments about its luxurious leather appointments from the guy who was going to pass or fail me. I failed the driving test and to this day I remember them saying, 'mirror, signal and manoeuvre'. The other thing was the use of the handbrake. This was the emergency brake and I was told that when parking one should press the button and raise it without any ratchet noise.

There was a separate test for Highway Code, which was much more advanced than Queensland's. Mostly I remember that part of the test which was for an emergency. Despite advance knowledge that this would happen during the test drive, I was still taken by surprise when the tester suddenly hit the dashboard with a rolled up newspaper he had probably read over morning tea. This was to indicate a possible collision. I had to brake immediately and keep the car under control, that is to say, in a straight line. Brake lock-up mechanisms (ABS) were still a thing of the future, as was automatic starting without using a choke. It was also taught that in winter, braking by using the gears was the way to go. This made sense as a way to avoid uncontrolled skids. They stopped short of a rear handbrake turn.

My pride was really damaged but I took some consolation in the fact that the daughter of Harry Secombe had failed, my inspector companion adding it was inevitable when being tested in a Rolls Royce. At least she had a chauffeur to drive her home.

As for me, I still had a few weeks to go on my international licence as the twelve months ticked towards the expiry date.

A few days later, with ice on the roads at QMH, I did a cold start with the choke a little far out and I could see the petrol and antifreeze burning off as fumes issued from the mufflers. I started to lose control as braking was ridiculous with the accelerator effectively half down. I applied the hand brake, pushed the choke in and slid gently into a visitor's parked car. A feeling of helplessness enveloped me as I realised I could not get out on the driver's side. I was completely parallel to the other car, in the sleet and black ice.

I turned off the ignition, scrambled across to the passenger side and almost broke a leg on the ice as the car's owner appeared after visiting a relative.

I stood in the freezing January cold after causing this accident with my second test a couple of weeks away. The rather tall expressionless owner of the other car approached and to my astonishment we found we could slide my car away from his. There was little damage to his vehicle and mine only had the rear bumper out of alignment.

We exchanged details and when I explained who I was the whole scenario changed as he realised I might be able to give him access to out of hour's visits, which he required because of the nature of his job. He was a driving instructor at the same venue where I had failed my first test.

Taught never to say sorry as it can be regarded as an admission of guilt, we talked and came to mutually acceptable arrangements. I sorted out his visits and gave him some cash which he could pocket rather than do any needless repairs, and I would sort myself out. This sorting included some lessons he offered as part of the deal, and arranging to have my final test taken with an instructor in a more comfortable environment.

I passed on my third attempt and felt I had learnt a lot. Perhaps this was the precursor to a business future.

* * *

Around this time a somewhat sensual interlude occurred in my room after drinks at the club with a medical student mate who was down for block work from London.

The adage that girls should never trust an intern or medical student where relationships were concerned was well and truly put to the test – thanks to a somewhat promiscuous final year student nurse and a school leaver she had taken under her wing to see if she would like to do nursing after high school. She, the younger of the two, oozed with natural beauty, with golden hair and tinted skin to match. She willingly lay upon my bed as I hesitantly lay next to her with my shoes still on.

The other two were on the floor on the dusty cheap carpet where she had no qualms about getting her knickers and tights pulled down and virtually off. She spread her legs in anticipation. I felt a shove followed by a request to know where my condoms were. I had none – a response that seemed not to worry either of them as he satisfied himself while she groaned in satisfaction. As she pulled up her pants, they caught some sperm and that was that. The episode left them both satisfied with him pulling off my shoes and encouraging me to follow their example.

This beautiful girl lay vulnerable in my arms but, without condoms, the chances of pregnancy was something I was not going to risk. She was unsophisticated and had lost her virginity to another boy back home, to whom she was contemplating becoming engaged.

We spent the night together with no dry sex but simply discussing life in general, her future and so on. She was clearly uneducated in many skills but deserved respect, as her mother and father would also expect. The next day, I met the other girl on the way to lunch and she asked me what I had done to her companion as she had written a Dear John letter to break off her engagement.

I said we had just talked and I never saw her again, though she wrote in immature handwriting inviting me to visit her in Kent. I did not reply. I often wondered why I didn't; but life is about choices.

I was soon to make my own choice in life, which, like education choices, can be right or wrong.

* * *

THERE WAS MUCH THAT I was to learn about Dorset and what a beautiful county it is.

Dorset is known for its Jurassic Coast. It features in books written by such wonderful scribes as Thomas Hardy and Jane

Austen with their wonderful descriptive accounts of all the Westcountry.

On our approach to her family home, on the outskirts of Parkstone, it was as if Gillian had read my thoughts. Or was it because I exclaimed, 'Do you live in this area?' I already knew what council houses, built for working class families, looked like, especially in the Midlands and the north of England. In London, because of the denser population, they manifested as desolate high-rises.

I received some sort of rebuke as our speed reduced and suburbia greeted us with its flashing red-brick buildings, bus stops, and green and red double-decker buses. We were heading due south after driving almost straight ahead at the Ringwood roundabout, ignoring the signs to Bournemouth and Ringwood and taking the turning towards Poole.

Gillian had pointed earlier to the miles of unspoilt land going back to ancient times and explained that this was the New Forest, designated as an Area of Outstanding Natural Beauty. She said numerous ponies roamed there and we could have a look. There were also plenty of pubs tucked away within this huge open space. With the odd bit of gorse and its somewhat stunted trees, the forest reminded me of home, and a tear or two welled in my eyes.

We came up to the top of a steep hill, with a pub and newsagent on the corner, and went straight ahead, descending the rather steep slope of Constitution Hill. A sharp first left at the bottom brought us to Harbour View Road. Number thirty-three, Gillian's home, was the second house on the right but I overshot so we had to turn around at the next junction and drive back to where Gillian's mother was waiting with roses and daffodils from the garden in hand.

Monica, as I eventually tested the waters to address her, was complete with apron and a lovely somewhat excited smile. No doubt this was at seeing Gillian, whereas for me it was politeness and probably thinking, *Good heavens, she has brought this Australian, home* whom she was curious to find out all about.

I fumbled nervously getting out the luggage and shopping bags. Gillian had bought some washing home, as daughters tend to do. To my surprise, I was later asked if I had any washing as she put a load into the front-loading washing machine in the kitchen.

They had an AGA and it was not long before Gillian was sitting on the bench next to it, Monica fussing around. I found a small chair to sit on and allow my heart to slow down.

This was a favourite spot for Monica as well, and a place where tea towels were spread to dry. The coal-fired heating was outside between the kitchen-cum-pantry and single-car garage.

The warmth of the greeting and the cosiness of the house put paid to the feeling of heading towards a cold and uninspiring council house.

The ground floor consisted of a separate dining room, toilet near the front door, storage under the staircase and a lovely lounge room with bay windows facing Poole Harbour to complete the feeling of cosiness and warmth. A fireplace, complete with mantlepiece and a French clock, happily ticked away as the afternoon sun streamed in. The fragrance of Brasso and furniture oil-cum-Goddard's silver cleaner pervaded the house. There was plenty of silver and brass to clean.

The pale blue carpet had been freshly hoovered, which was quite a feat in a house without open planning.

Showing me to my room up the narrow staircase was Gillian's responsibility, albeit a fleeting one as she dived into her own room to throw open thick curtains behind a tiny, well-appointed dressing table. All three bedrooms had built-in wardrobes. The toilet and adjoining bathroom were decorated in the black and green typical of the period. Especially noted was the separate toilet as I had a thing about privacy in that respect. A small window allowed viewing and ventilation with a thin wispy curtain for privacy. As I had a much-needed pee I could see from the window my white Rover TC parked outside and the houses across the road. Cars went up and down Constitution Hill, whereas Harbor View Road was relatively quiet.

I quickly assumed any thoughts of being in the same room as Gillian were not the order of the day. She had the smaller bedroom, by choice, I believe, of the two siblings' bedrooms. By now, Monica was in the larger room (Angela's) with me, opening the right-hand side of one of the built-in wardrobes and pushing hanging dresses to one side to make room for my clothes. I explained I would be happy living out of my suitcase, whereupon she showed me lovely folded fresh towels upon the bed, one of two facing a semi-bay window and the harbour. Two steps up the staircase was the master bedroom.

Most of the doors were ajar, which I assumed was to retain the heat of the day and provide warmth at night. At the top of the stairs was a boiler cupboard for drying clothes or keeping them warm.

Walls were traditionally decorated with wallpaper, paintings and memorable prints also thoughtfully hung.

I did not take in all this detail at the time, but my strong memory of the house correctly suggests life-changing events were to unfold, which meant this would not be my only visit there with the smiling, bubbly and somewhat radical Gillian.

A large plate, covered in foil, sat atop the AGA, and I detected the smell of fish. This was a time when marked differences were still evident between Roman Catholics and those of Church of England faith.

The sound of garage doors closing heralded the return home of Peter Rowley Brooks, husband to Monica and father of Gillian and Angela. Monica greeted him at the side door to the kitchen and I heard muffled voices as I sat in the lounge with Gillian. Peter came in and introduced himself to this young beau of his youngest daughter. The evening meal would soon be served after drinks and a chat. I probably had a beer and Peter certainly had a Scotch on the rocks, adding some ice from a small fridge in the pantry. Drinks were taken at this time on a Friday, but nowadays I show contempt for such societal-controlled behaviour.

We went into the usual perfunctory discussions that occur when people are tired at the end of the week, or meeting for the first time: polite conversation, getting to know each other, chatting.

Gillian eventually sat on the floor at her father's feet as he reclined in his quintessentially English man's chair. Clearly, Gillian was close to her family, especially to Peter.

Although it was too early to envisage a serious future together, thoughts of the reality flashed through my mind. Here I was wearing velvet cords and sitting making conversation in the fading light in a lounge room in a country far from Australia.

With but a few shirts to my name and the odd pairs of socks salvaged from hospital laundries in St Mary's in London, it was impossible to contemplate how the future would unfold if our relationship developed. Though I had a profession that guaranteed a relatively substantial income and a car parked outside, a relationship was as difficult to surmise as actually parking in the garage where an Opel car was cooling down beside the omnipresent freezer.

The freezer was to be used quite a lot as Monica, a post Second World War housewife, had discovered frozen meals made considerable cost-effective sense.

Because the freezer was not frost free Monica was often found in the garage chipping away at it regardless of the season. Carrying hot water with steam rising from the bowl was frightening, to say the least. I doubt whether she would be convinced to actually have a frost free one when they became available. I rarely went into the garage as the door was so difficult to lock and unlock; then to lift it was almost sure to give one a hernia. But it didn't seem to bother Monica. The clothesline, accessed via the steps towards the pond at the back, consisted of a forked pole to hold up the line. There was a tool shed under the house which often held bulbs to be planted in the appropriate season.

When the wind suddenly blew in off the English Channel, or the clouds became heavy with rain, Monica would scurry on down to retrieve the damp or dry clothes, before they were infected with itchy grass cuttings or even an occasional dropping from those pesky foxes that lived in the area and had a lair in the bush at Constitution Hill. Peter had a clutch-driven drum-roller mower which he used in summer to make the lawn look great. With the sun beaming down, it reminded me of Wimbledon grass, but of course was not tifdwarf.

Fallen leaves were the bane of Monica's gardening life. She stockpiled them towards the back fence and had an occasional burn-off, remembering it was paramount to keep the windows closed against the billowing smoke and make sure there was nothing on the clothesline.

A large maple tree bordered the view from the lounge out towards the neighbours' large white stucco house and the road to Poole from Constitution Hill. The tree was really beautiful in autumn when the changing colour of its leaves heralded the change of seasons. In summer, the tree provided cooling shade, particularly to the lounge room.

A small vegetable garden with cos lettuce, spring onions and radishes was often an early summer planting. Herbaceous plants were more to the other side, with rosemary, basil and thyme on the border with the other neighbour. That was where the most beautiful bay tree also grew, without any attention needed. Monica always picked her own bay leaves, drying them near the oven. This made for delicious casseroles, made from ingredients, not a packet, and simmered for hours. I loved her coq au vin so much it will never be forgotten. Dried bay leaves would find their way to airtight jars stored in the pantry for use when required in a recipe.

A typical summer lunch would be a pork pie, with Branston pickle, cheeses, shallots and bread. Mustard, such as Dijon, was my favourite and later became a contentious issue in regard to expiry dates.

Monica enjoyed a gin and tonic, which she quaffed between running to the kitchen and back from her seat in the lounge. Offered another, she told Peter she was about to serve the meal. He had a little mutter-cum-giggle into his glass as he finished pouring his second Scotch and suggested a bottle of wine with the meal. The question of white or red was discussed and Monica suggested, as she was serving fish, white would be more appropriate. I said I didn't mind, gulped as I said even a beer would do, then thought better of it as we were ushered into the dining room. Everyone had their particular chair, and on the sideboard were silverware and ornaments.

It looked as if the table could be extended. My seat was with the back to the window and a small terrace, with Gillian sitting to my right. I gathered I was sitting in Angela's chair, who was in London and I was still to meet. I probably had not heard of plaice (the British term for flounder) or Dover sole (a high-end flounder). It was absolutely delicious and accompanied by an Australian wine clearly showing they were very welcoming. Capers floated around in the butter sauce and the grilled fish was cooked to perfection. When I complimented Monica on the fish, she commented, 'We were not sure whether you were a Roman Catholic so, as it is Friday, we thought it was a nice choice', or words to that effect.

'Actually I am Church of England,' I said, casting my mind back to confirmation at St Thomas Church of England at Toowong, now known as Anglican and heritage listed.

Raspberries and cream followed with a choice of ice-cream. Sometimes Monica would serve Devonshire clotted cream, which was absolutely delicious.

* * *

AFTER WHAT CAN BE a very cold and wet winter in the UK, the coming of spring heralds bright new life – bluebells, snowdrops, with jonquils and daffodils and the opportunity to pick wild berries.

Wild mushrooms are often gathered, but this takes a bit of learning, as the poisonous mushrooms can be deadly. I have not done much wild picking of fruit; at that time of my life our meals were rich in meat foods, custard and tinned fruit.

As Poole is only a short journey across the English Channel from Roscoff and Brittany in northern France summer meant the arrival of the 'Onion Johnnies'. Wearing a traditional striped shirt and beret, these Frenchmen pedalled and pushed bicycles laden with strings of onions that they hawked to households throughout southern England.

This was their cash income, the bikes their only transport. Because of the poor postwar infrastructure in northern France, getting to England was a better bet than trying to get to Paris. They also brought garlic but mostly it was those sweet white onions, suitable to be chewed as well as used in salads. And they could be warehouse stored. Nowadays, they may well be decorations in country pubs, and in Europe's Mediterranean countries, dried chillies are a similar tradition, especially Italy.

***

THE REST OF OUR first weekend in Poole was spent sightseeing.

A trip through lower Parkstone and a drive under the one-way rail bridge brought us to Poole Park, with its steam train mini railway chuffing around. Opposite was low-level land, which contained some sort of lake, which to this day, I still do not know its purpose, nor did the black and white swans care a tinker's cuss, happily gliding by. Canada geese were also there walking around the lake's edge. A father and son were enjoying sailing and others were flying kites. Sculptured garden beds and green lawns gave the opportunity to lay out an invariably red-chequered rug to avoid the damp as they picnicked on whatever food they had brought with them. Children and adults were playing on a couple of free bitumen tennis courts. Invariably present in most picnic parks was an ice-cream van, and a small shop selling anything from small packets of Smarties to fairy floss (cotton candy in the US).

We drove on down to lower Poole, which was known as Poole Quays. Wispy smoke was emerging from a chimney where people were queuing to enter a factory-like building.

This was the long-established Poole Pottery factory, very popular throughout the country for its distinctive patterned design. Its pieces are now very collectible and well worth having. Not quite on the scale as Clarice Cliff, but nevertheless well renowned.

Family

*Grandchildren together, Jackson Horse Riding and with Wally Lewis
:Peter winning in Toronto Cottingham Tennis Club: December 7th 2014
NOW TOP OF THE TENNIS CHALLENGE TABLE Winter
Club Events.*

*Graded by Resident Professionals Peter realized eventually he
was* **RATED 5.5.** *It is of little consequence to him as he just enjoys
playing.* **5.5 Rating means:-** *You have mastered power and/or consistency
as a major weapon. You can vary strategies and styles of play in a
competitive situation and hit dependable shots in a stress situation.*

6.0 to 7.0. *You have had intensive training for national tournament
competition at the junior and collegiate levels and have obtained a sectional
and/or national ranking.*

7.0: You are a world-class player.

℞ Bacteriostats and Anti-Virals

St Mary's Paddington Praed St London (circa 2014)

Penicillin *is the wonder drug of its time and continues to save so many lives, as the molecular structure is reshaped to form other* **anti-bacterial derivatives** *of what is called the* **Penicillin Family.**

Anti-Viral: Coved-19 *pharmaceuticals were developed at Oxford and Cambridge University UK which have saved millions of lives Astra Zeneca and* **Pfizer in USA** *all contributed. Even at UQ, research was advanced which was withdrawn, for Therapeutic reasons.*

Paxlovid by Pfizer =nirmatrelvir 150mg (Figure Left) +ritonavir 100mg (Figure Right) (NIH, NationalLibrary of Medicine et al)

Molecular Structures as recommended sources PDF, Wiki, et al. Illustrative here for purposes of defining Molecular structures, as in **Pharmaceutical Chemistry. Formulae available in Texts**

Family (Except the Crocodile)

Figure (Left) *Sara and Jackson and Jackson Oscar:* **Middle (Right)** *Cooper and Zoe at private school in UK.*
& Top Right: *never smile at a crocodile, especially an albino one!*

Figure: Vietnam (Conscription)

"Rolling the dice" Top Left Conscription in Australia.
Vietnam Museum Phillip Island Victoria Australia

Figure: *Author's Vietnam Rising Sun and Medals*

**U Q Jacaranda's St Lucia Campus :
Examination Time October 22nd 2017**

*Ranked 39th in the World for Science 2017 McGill and Toronto Much Higher
Oxford not far away though. Harvard # 1 Thanks to UQ News to Rod*

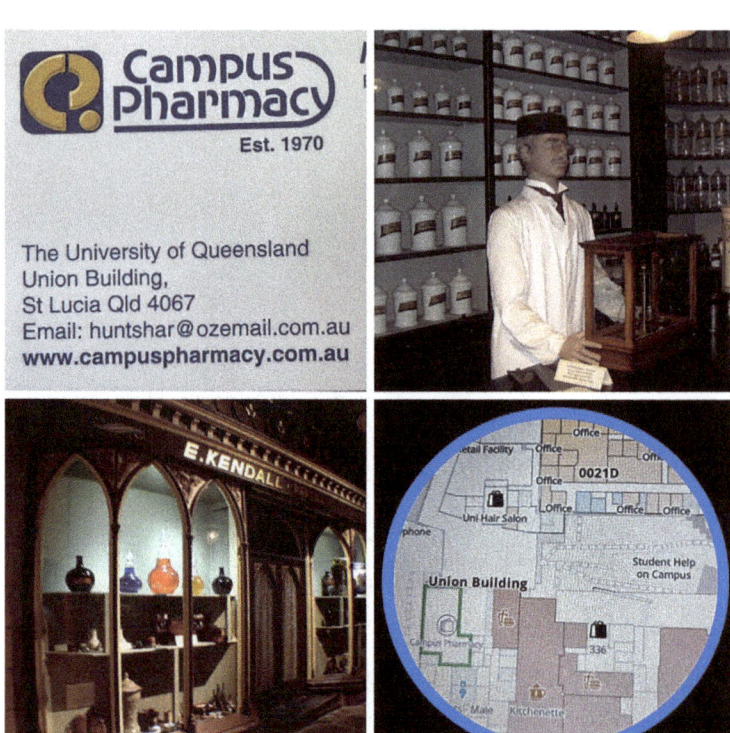

Top Left Business Card. **Top** Pharmacy in **Folklore Museum**, which is a restored 17th Century *****Almshouse**, used to belong to cobbler's guild. Also was displayed a classroom, cobbler's workshop confectionary, tailor etc. **July2007** Kirkgate Victorian Pharmacy at the **York Museum:** York UK *****Béguinage** is similar. **Bottom** Left. E. Kendall Apothecary with window display. **Bottom** Right.

The location of Campus Pharmacy: as is shown in the University of Queensland Plans Union Footprint.

Theme:-The Journey through to Campus Pharmacy 1970 (Author) Historic Photos by Author

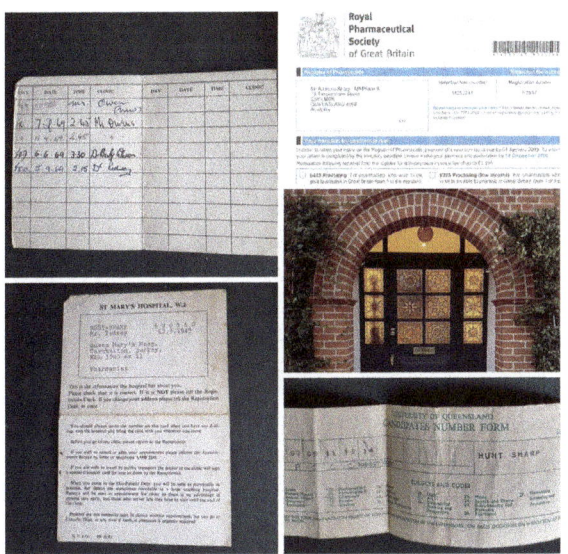

London: *St Mary's and Queen Mary's Simulated Sick Bay entrance.*

Top Right *MPS (GB) under Royal Charter*
Bottom Right *UQ Entrance Matriculation*

(Photographer Gillian)
The bridge over the River Thames has a themed "Red Colour" representing the House of Lords whilst the bridge upriver has a green colour motif matching the leather seats of the House of Commons. Jan (deceased and also Mary Liz circa: (**Coved Pandemic**) *told us this before afternoon tea and a tour of the Houses of Parliament and viewing the Parliamentary Houses.*
Wishing you a **Very Happy Christmas** *and a fantastic 2015*
With best wishes from Jan and Mary Liz

East India Club

Sat 23/03/2013 1:46 AM SIMON, J Viscount SIMONJ@parliament.uk
Dear Rod and Gillian, We would love to have dinner with you on 7th May at your club – many thanks for inviting us. The afternoon of Wednesday, 5th June, would be a good day for you to come to the House of Lords and we'll discuss timing when we see you in May.

With best wishes, Jan and Mary Liz

The Royal Britannia Museum Leith Scotland 2nd September 2007

With the Britannia and its opulence and history behind, I was surprised and pleased that the Royal Barge was also here. The Royal Barge was used for transferring the Royal Family to land from the Britannia where Ports were shallow.

My interest in the Royal Barge was that it was on this very Queen's Barge that I had travelled as the lead boat up the Thames during the **Thames River Pageant** around 1968-69. It was also where I had had my first Gin and Tonic, as a young man where the measure from the then Harbour Master was appropriate in a Naval sense: accompanied by cucumber sandwiches, as the fireworks exploded above this lead boat.

Anecdotally: I was almost seasick at the time from the wake 0f the flotilla of boats at the time!!

Queensland Government House *Visit 3rdApril 2024*

Nelson's (MBE) 1972 Silver Cloud Seychelles Blue with King Charles Monarchy Crown Middle Left Cooper currently on Crutches.

Queen Elizabeth's II Personal RR Standard 1982 Brisbane Commonwealth Games

Testimonial

"I hope to be in touch soon regarding your upcoming 60-Year Reunion of the Class of 1962. We are still planning next year's calendar of events, but 14 May has been set aside as a tentative date for the 60-year reunion celebration.

Thank you for your great voiceover contribution to our Giving Day video. We managed to meet and exceed our goal of $300,000 on the day, all thanks to the wonderful generosity of our BBC parents, Old Boys and friends. I did hear from Philip Korn, and sent him details of how he can make a contribution from the USA."

Kind regards,

Carol Stephens | Community Engagement Manager | Brisbane Boys' College

Kensington Terrace | Toowong | Queensland 4066 | Australia

T +61 07 3309 3526 | M 0416 085 136

E cstephens@bbc.qld.edu.au | W www.bbc.qld.edu.au

A school of the Presbyterian and Methodist Schools' Association (PMSA) | CRICOS 00491J

Figure 2 Memorial Seats Author Achieved with Brisbane City Council

Anzac Memorial Seats, Keating Park, Indooroopilly Brisbane

7 July 2023 Mr Rod Hunt-Sharp 35 Verney Road West GRACEVILLE QLD 4075 Dear Mr Hunt-Sharp Thank you for your email of 8 June 2023 about the War Memorial at Keating Park, Indooroopilly. The Lord Mayor is currently away from the office and has asked that I reply on this occasion. Every day, Council works with residents and local communities to make sure the Brisbane of tomorrow is even better than the Brisbane of today. I acknowledge that memorial parks hold a special significance for many people in the community and appreciate your request for seating to be provided for people who may wish to sit and reflect in the area of the War Memorial. In light of your suggestion, Mr Ted Krosman, Parks Planning Coordinator from City Standards, was asked to consider your request and I am pleased to advise that three park benches will be installed in Keating Park, at the Coonan Street and Belgrave Street corner. It is anticipated this work will be completed by the end of August. I trust this information is of assistance to you. Should you have any further queries about this matter, please questions, Mr Krosman can be reached on 3407 0841. Thank you for taking the time to raise this matter.

Yours sincerely Krista Adams ACTING MAYOR Ref: LM02069-2023

NOVEMBER FIVE MINUTE SPEAKER: Rodney Hunt-Sharp
PROBUS CLUB OF CHAPEL HILL INC
NEWSLETTER January 2014 - VOL 6 NO 9

Newsletter Editor: Peter Dahm

Five minute speaker Rodney (Rod) Hunt-Sharp began his talk by referencing "Little Boy", that infamous atomic bomb which was dropped on Hiroshima in the dying days of WW11. But, as his talk developed and he gave an account of his work experience in various hospitals in the UK, his broader message about the good that can be found in otherwise dreadful and unexpected situations became evident.

Rod explained that being born shortly after WW11 he did not directly experience any of those activities as a youngster, although he did see a lot of reminders as he grew up. He too was called up for service (in Vietnam), but was later turned down on health grounds, and was later diagnosed with renal TB. This was while he was working at Queen Mary's Hospital for Children in Carshalton, Surrey. He was successfully treated in St Mary's Paddington Hospital, and commented that this was the best place to be with the rather rare renal TB as it was a renowned renal hospital.

It was at St Mary's and Queen Mary's Hospitals that Rod enjoyed the warmth of the staff at Christmas, and he commented that he would always remember the Head of Surgery carving the turkey on the ward. Invited to the Christmas drinks in a spare theatre and to the Mikado, the Medical School pantomime, his stay was a bit like a Carry-On movie at times. Rod related an anecdote about unsuccessfully endeavouring to obtain a driver's licence while in England. He had been turned down a few times until he met the examiner at Queen Mary's in unusual circumstances. He accidentally slid his car on ice outside a ward at QM into a visitor's car. Lo and behold, it belonged to the very examiner who later gave him lessons to help him pass the driving test; yet another case of good shining through perhaps?

He met wife to be Gillian while working at Queen Mary's Hospital for Children, which also specialised in Spina Bifida. While there he recalled doing the Christmas rounds, and being pressed to have a glass of sherry at each ward, putting his newly acquired UK driving licence at real risk. From Carshalton, Rod moved to the Poole General in Dorset, where he was promoted to Deputy Chief Pharmacist. In charge of Sterile Dispensing, he recalled the visit to the unit to prepare intravenous food for a **little baby boy**. It was an opportunity to provide the family with their first Christmas dinner together. Rod recalled the wonderful touch of Christmas Cheer when a nurse placed fresh holly around the IVF Bottle, as the family gathered for Christmas Lunch with their **little boy**. Repeating his observation that good can often be found in what is otherwise a bad situation; Rod concluded his talk by wishing everyone a Merry Christmas, with the plea to spare a thought and a prayer for the suffering. PS The Chairperson commented it was exactly 5 minutes in duration. Amazing!

TENNIS

FIGURES PLUS TESTIMONIAL

Top: *Author playing at Tennyson Tennis Centre; temporary boards were put down with clay on top, for a ladies tournament previously played.*

Top Right Father and son winning 6/0/6/2 at Tatts Tennis. (note ball in photo).

Bottom Centre: *Author, Peter, Cooper, "Hunt-Sharp Tennis Dynasty" The first email is referring to Cooper, Peter and myself as a Photo Insert in the Tattersalls Tennis Programme calendar.*

From: *Robert & Joal Gardner [mailto:robert.joal@bigpond.com]*
Sen Sat 21/01/2012 6:48 PM

To: *Rod Hunt-Sharp*

From one GOB to the Supreme *GOB (*my pseudonym for Grumpy Old Bastard)

You are too fast for me H-S ..... on and off the court

I will be sending out a bulk email in the next week to advise of no tennis next Thursday And as I have your attention I wish to advise that the 3G photo of the H-S dynasty will appear in the 2012 edition of our Programme.... I assume that I do not need your approval Regards Bob

Testimonials

From: Robert & Joal Gardner [mailto:robert.joal@bigpond.com]
Sent: Thursday, 27 November 2014 10:32 AM
To: Rod Hunt-Sharp
Subject: Re: RACQUETEERS

It's so nice to deal with a person of real class On and off the court

Bob

Bob Gardiner was the then Secretary of Tattersalls' Racqueteers. Old Boy of BSHS *Below refers to the Doubles Final which was a record for the club. It was in excess of 4 hours. My partner and I were on -30 points for each game, as I recall.*

Those kind but misguided readers who have squandered their time in ploughing through previous editions of this report will have come to the realization that its connection with tennis has been at best peripheral and tenuous, if not non-existent, being predicated on the theory that our tennis contests have scant appeal to the wider Club Membership.

Regrettably there are phases in the life of the Racqueteers where little of note occurs, so we are confronted with the unpalatable choice of turning the focus of this report, as a last resort, to the noble game of tennis, a novel, perhaps unique occurrence.

Every year we conduct the Peter Geraghty Memorial Doubles Handicap, where the names of all participants are drawn randomly and the pairings are then assigned a handicap. This challenging task inevitably meets with trenchant criticism from those who perceive that their chances of success have been hampered by the onerous and grievously unfair burden imposed upon them by the poor benighted handicappers, who happen to be the four Committee Members. Such slings as are directed at them are normally borne with stoic calm, but occasionally their collective wisdom is so manifest that even the most mean spirited and self-interested are forced to vouchsafe their sublime skill and judgement in assigning handicaps so accurate that the outcome of a match is so close as to defy prediction.

Such an occasion arose with this year's final, which pitted a pair of highly experienced campaigners Gary Tupicoff and Rod Hunt-Sharp against last year's runner-up Jon Hogan and his prodigal son partner Warren Porter, who having left the fold for quite a few years had this year, after much derision from his mates, finally renewed his Tatts Membership, thereby rendering him eligible to play in Racqueteers tournaments again.

And so it came to pass that a match which began at lunchtime, dragged on for over four hours and had to be concluded under lights.

Umpiring such a protracted and at times acrimonious and ill-tempered contest, particularly one involving a handicap scoring method, was calculated to test the resolve and endurance of even the most sanguine of temperaments, but court captain Kos Psaltis selflessly offered himself up to this most thankless and challenging of causes and performed to an exemplary standard. (It is expected that such fulsome praise will cement his occupancy of this role in all future finals.)

In a superb demonstration of the handicappers' craft, the longest match in the Club's history played itself out to a 3-6 11-9 7-5 win with Jon and Warren eventually emerging victorious.

A commendable number of the Racqueteers remained in the gathering darkness to witness the denouement of this Homeric struggle as these aged and wearied warriors finally staggered from the courts to a no doubt well-earned rest. It being by this stage well past their bed time.

Tatts Magazine Circa 2014, Article in larger Print

Gillian, Author, with Scott Kelly; who was an Astronaut with a Twin.

Racism & Multiculturalism

Author's Depictions of Multiculturism

Top *As photographed at New York Museum of Modern Art (Men's Bathroom)*
Bottom *Amber Light at Glasgow Central Rail Station*

Around 10.00PM in Glasgow centre it is fairly quiet, except at the "one up" nightclub which was right across from our room in the **Western Club.** *There was one bashing during the day and a crime scene set up just outside, but for this, not entirely a lot really happens. Come Friday night though it is time to party. This caricature shot shows the Bag Piper and West Indian/African Bongo Players busking as if they had done it forever with the syncing of harmony. Note the Muslim woman behind. Talk about diversity! The Glasgow Royal Concert Hall is in the background. Please note amber light, a colourful blending.*

Top photo: *acknowledges the Caboolture Historical Society **ca. 1920s** Attewell's Mill Trade March Collector; Sampson Frank.* **Bottom Left:** *Rod walking (opening day) and talking whilst avoiding bicycles on the expensive walkway on the banks of the Brisbane River **May 2021**; this is near the Art Deco Indooroopilly Suspension Bridge (Walter Taylor **circa 1936**).* **Upper Right** *from Rod: European Bicycle Stockholm outside George Jensen Shop.* **Lower Left:** *my Uncle Jesse Stanley Hunt FASA photo **ca1980**.* **Bottom Right:** *He purchased a Ford Zephyr which he changed to from bicycle riding to Attewell's Mill on retirement: the Picture represents a typical Zephyr (circa 1980's web sourced model).*

Upper *Brisbane Boys' College:* **Down:** *Rosedale Police Station:* **Bottom** *Taringa State School (Demolished) Established circa 1900. Morrow Street. To the Right not shown were Bitumin Tennis Courts Championship Size. (Qld Government Archives)*
https://trove.nla.gov.au/newspaper/article/22153875

Brisbane Boys' College
Photo: **Upper:** *BBC Captain 1991 Peter Hunt-Sharp talking to a student after talking with his maths teacher still at BBC Chicca Masoud (now deceased) 16.07.21*
Middle *"Let Honour Stainless Be" Sit Sine Labe Decus*

Photograph by the Author at Bournemouth Beach UK

Above *Striped Colours: The one is larger on the left. What could this mean? Perhaps it applies to* **Physical Chemistry?**

Courier Mail Brisbane Edition

Houses

Bowaga Street Figure 2 Chapel Hill

Old Marcoola Beach House 2022

Flindersia Street Marcoola.

Kensington Terrace

Pullenvale House
Same Flats next to our demolished house
91 Harts Road Indooroopilly.

Twickenham St Chelmer

Taringa Police Station

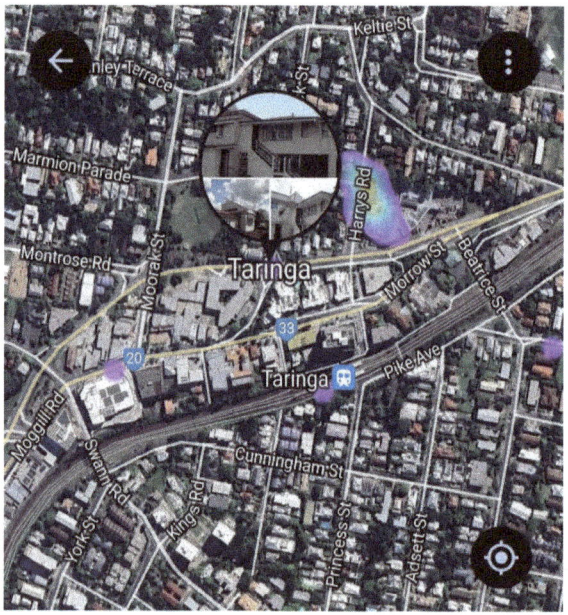

Taringa Police Station: Brisbane, Queensland.

Top: Blue Dot   Back Entrance to the Police Office (Kitchen above Office).

Orange Dot   Storage Area for Files and used as a Pretend Jail area for play.

Green Dot   Dining Room.

Red Dot   Picket Fence where my father was pinned, and I made a Citizen's Arrest.

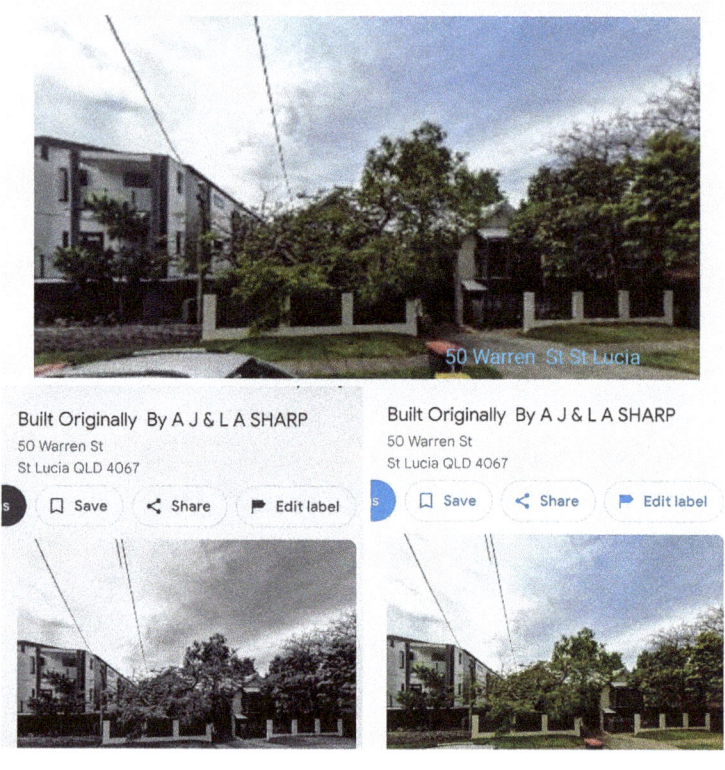

*50 Warren Street St Lucia as marked
(now Units for Students and Staff)*

Logos

'logos' means science or study.

Maltese Cross
University of Queensland
[My personal one]

Griffith University
Coat of Arms

Current Griffith
University logo

During the Commonwealth Games the Coat of Arms was the only thing we were licensed to sell with Royalties going to the University. The Logo only appeared much later, and was never used to my knowledge during the Commonwealth Games Memorabilia Sales (See Later)

This Logo for the Commonwealth Games we found to be the most acceptable for souvenir purchases for athletes from around the Commonwealth of Nations. There was no way of knowing this, when vast orders of Memorabilia were made by Gillian. (See also the International Stick Pins Pictures with their Logos.

This is traditional sign for
Recipe in Latin Prescriptions

MARRIED LIFE

We had had two choices once married. We could stay in the UK which would, because of government regulations, cause me bother to be able to stay long term, despite all the positives it brought to the UK. There were thousands entering illegally and legally from all parts of the UK's previously colonised world. They were welcomed, as every history student would know, as it was the humanitarian and jolly right thing to do for these people.

It was abundantly clear that these newcomers were mostly attracted by the free health system which they did not have in their own countries. The positive side was that they were willing to do menial jobs that others shunned.

But that was the UK and not Australia, which had a white Australia policy from the time of the crucial postwar resettlement. We had migration of the Irish (potato famine), Italians (probably unemployed but useful in Cairns), Greeks (small business devotees), Anglo Saxons (UK folk who were sick of the West Indian and African influx) and Chinese (back to the gold-rush era). After Vietnam, we had a conscience appeal to many displaced by communism in that country's south, although never was consideration given to the demographic necessities.

Our voyage home ended gliding up the Brisbane River, its entrance lined with mangroves as I talked about the mud crabs, explaining what they were to Gillian.

Walking down the gangplank was another surreal experience. Here we were with very little cash, disembarking for a new life in all respects in Brisbane.

After we passed through Customs a large amount of luggage joined us as we looked around anxiously and with anticipation. Nelson and Gillian met for the first time. I remember little of the occasion and was probably focused on the relatively short journey to Warren Street, St Lucia, where my parents were waiting.

That was an unusual surprise, with warmth and affection seemingly all round. My mother, Alma, was anxious to talk to me on her own about her problems, rather than solve them with husband Bert. Well, why did I expect this? Simply because it had never been any different, as I had been singled out as the unmarried youngest sibling to be a recipient of emotions that had dogged me all my life.

What I did not know was that it was just the beginning and Gillian had to be protected. I was responsible for supporting her as we had virtually nothing, with all or most of our goods and chattels still on their way thanks to the help of John Simon, someone who Gillian's father had never really warmed to.

Our wedding present from my parents was very nice as it was some money and a lovely double bed set up in one of their bedrooms. Oops! They meant well but we were already looking to see where we could rent as privacy was paramount. But it was all they could do, not knowing our circumstances of having been at sea and in the days when contact was by telegram, using Morse code. Those days, rental was far less difficult than now. It was not long before we found a flat at Augustus Street, Toowong, near the railway line and the central area now housing the Toowong Village shopping centre. We still go there every week for groceries and the occasional trip to the bank. It is now a cosmopolitan place with the unit at the top of the six-pack block into which, not long after our arrival, we moved all our goods and chattels while I began to look for a Job. Pharmacists were in short supply, especially those with my considerable experience and registered in two countries.

I soon found an assistant manager's job at the T&G Day and Night Pharmacy, smack bang in the middle of city central in Queen Street where there is now a mall with the Tattersalls Club at the other end where some few years later I became a member.

After the hospital pay rates in the UK, I was pleasantly surprised at the wage I received. It was a busy pharmacy, where upstairs in the building were several commercial firms and the lawyers Morris Fletcher and Cross, which later became Minter Ellison, which we still engage today. (School captain for my year, Ric Clarke, was already a partner.)

While working at T&G I was in waiting mode to see what was happening about the proposed pharmacy on the UQ campus and what could be set in place. Gossip spreads quickly in all business circles, but none more so than in the world of pharmacy via the Pharmacy Guild's Queensland branch. The word was out that it was going to be tendered for and a likeable red-headed dude from the so-called pharmacy elite was a front runner but not to underestimate the Lefties at the UQ campus student union who favoured a friendly society pharmacy with free health for student members and reduced prescription costs.

My father had recently retired from the QPS and had known Bruce Green, UQ's deputy registrar. Part of his territory, or precinct, during several years as officer in charge of the Taringa police station had included the university. His charter was 'the protection of life and property' within that area. That oath continues today for any police officer graduating from the police academy.

This was a time when the university had its own by-laws as a statutory arrangement between the Commonwealth (the funder) and State government (custodial providers in Queensland). Once a year for several years, from around Christmas to approximately New Year's Eve, UQ would be closed off to the general public by lowering boom gates at its entrances. My father routinely checked on them as part of his responsibility.

Coincidently, when he retired, at around fifty-five years of age, the university, by way of Bruce Green, was becoming very aware of the need for additional security at the St Lucia campus. So my father was appointed as its first security officer, something that has never been acknowledged by the university, whether by political intent or sheer lack of understanding. Or perhaps it was in the category of decisions and moves made that are buried and never found. And any admission that UQ had appointed someone to be a conduit of information back to the state under a Bjelke-Petersen coalition government would be political dynamite. However, my father was appointed to check on various security aspects of the university, answering only and directly to Bruce Green who was then the conduit to the senate and vice chancellor.

The appointment continued for around a decade, and although some suspicion was held about his role by those in the Arts Faculty – and particularly by those lecturers and professors in government and international relations – nothing could be proved.

My parents had bought land at 50 Warren Street, St Lucia, which was where I lived during my time as a student. An astute businessperson, Dad finished up with a quarter of an acre of land and with one goal – to build a tennis court down the back. This he achieved by talking to soil removers at building sites at the university who gladly dropped fill into the swampy low backyard over a few years. This eventually became an entertainment area, albeit to the chagrin of my sister, Narelle. Tennis parties were great, largely taking the place of those at the Caboolture court as that house and court had by then been sold by Uncle Jesse.

* * *

UNREST WAS DEVELOPING ON all tertiary student campuses, stirred by a combination of the liberated freedom of the sixties when sex was now talked about and intelligent hippies became orators just like those of the Greco-Roman period. There were numerous toga parties at the university pub, and what went on or came off was nobody's business. Freedom and a fun time for all.

But there was also the Vietnam War, which affected me in a direct way with conscription starting a few years earlier. JFK had been assassinated so now was a time of US presidents such as Nixon and LBJ, and the domino theory about the advance of communism reigned and filled newspaper headlines. And none more so than the student union newspaper, *Semper Floreat*, which was the one read by students.

* * *

IMAGINE WORKING IN THE city and trying to clinch an agreement to open a pharmacy where this had not been done before. There was always the presence of self-doubt and pressure about being able to achieve the agreement to do that, especially when that was why we had returned to Australia.

It was touted to be an instant success with a captive audience of thousands of students who would be knocking on the door for service. But why would they, when the location was hidden at the rear of the student union building with its splendid view across the then ant bed tennis courts and the palms beside the Brisbane River, which formed a natural boundary for the beautiful campus?

Even if successful, who would be the lessor? This was to prove to be a very difficult journey to navigate between two major players – the student union (who were the primary advocates as I worked in the city T&G) and the University of Queensland, culminating in the senate which had the final say.

Fortunately I had a lovely final year pharmacist graduand who had transferred her registration necessities to me when I began as manager of the T&G Pharmacy. Her name was Darrien, a sensuous girl, who if I were to walk up to her today, I would probably click with like a brother. We had many discussions about UQ and she brought me up to speed about that. I tended to be distracted by the zip of her white coat as she leant across to help dispense prescriptions from some health service upstairs. This was quite unusual as in those days such services were always confined to urban strips in the suburbs. They largely still are, along with ancillary health care.

We talked about such care and felt that X-rays and the like were not on the campus, and never would be, so such services would be outsourced. I was aware that American campuses had large shopping centres, with a complete health care system. Gillian and I later visited these wherever possible to gain valuable insights into trends and their implementation.

Darrien still had the student mindset and when she listened to stories of my travels she hung on every word and adsorbed everything in an instant. She was clearly one very clever woman, who was destined for greater things than pharmacy, a person who thought long and hard about a particular point, before forming her considered opinion.

I learnt that within the student union building there was an addition called the relaxation block in which there were the beginnings of a rudimentary health service offering, including psychological counselling. But psychologists don't write scripts, then or now.

There are two parts to a retail pharmacy, the front shop and the dispensary. Now if the volume of NHS scripts or PBS, as they were to be soon known, was insufficient to make a crust then the registered pharmacist, who was then the only entitled owner, would go out of business if retail sales were not profitable. There was this left-wing mindset that said pharmacists were wealthy individuals, and the Marxist lefties in the union and academia sought some socialist alternative in the form of a friendly society. For some years I was followed and niggled (bullied), even in the men's urinal downstairs from the shop, with suggestions that I would be removed. That ended when the slimy bastard by the name of Fowler died prematurely from natural causes.

I had not studied politics or law, so I had to rely upon artificial tears as I approached negotiations with the then president of the union. Fortunately, he was a pharmacist with great ambitions to be an educator and would succumb to the right word. Some might call it flattery, but I would call it discretion.

It is really hard to describe what was going on; suffice to say that the process of receiving the right to have a pharmacy on the campus was very complicated with so many factions involved.

I got there with the guidance of a few aforementioned people and as the respected son of a policeman who was their security officer watching for bandits on pay days when large amounts of money were transferred from the Commonwealth Bank in the union building across to the J D Story Building. There were never any robberies, but with security in place it reassured everyone at the J D Story Building that they would get their fortnightly or monthly pay. The end of each month would be a double whammy for a robbery when monthly and fortnightly pays coincided.

As the pay system gravitated to EFT this became less of a problem and so my father inclined more towards reporting about the emerging radicalism occurring here and on campuses around the world. American campuses were alive with black movements, apartheid and Vietnam War atrocities with 'Bring them home' becoming the catchcry for riots and confrontational protests on both sides. Sadly, when the Vietnam War veterans did come home they were shunned by shameful behaviour from those you would expect would not be at all like that.

As always, what happens in social and business affairs in the USA eventually arrives in Australia, and when American President Lyndon Baines Johnson visited Australia, security was considerable. Off campus, security was looked after by ASIO and others, along with the CIA and US military. This has never changed, including the relatively recent visit to UQ by President Obama espousing a lack of knowledge of the real issues, with the then Governor General Quentin Bryce showing her admiration for this well-spoken lawyer from Chicago, who now lives and plays golf in Hawaii. Black, like Martin Luther King, he was never as good an orator as King. But he came close, with the power of the White House and Congress behind him.

Air Force One was parked at Amberley air force base near Ipswich for his stay. Johnson might well have done the same with the crowds whipped up into a frenzy by the slogan, 'All the way with LBJ'.

Police forces in most states had in those times what were

known as special branches attached to them. My father was never a member of such a unit, though many radicals suspected he may well have been and when he was around they were very careful about what they said and did. Were they right? We will never know. However, his name was Sergeant Sharp, whereas mine was Hunt-Sharp, which happily was a loose connection.

He never came near the pharmacy, but we often communicated on the home landline during his lunch hour when things were extremely important. It was dangerously open to the wrong interpretation, but passed the time away when people were paranoid about communists under the bed and the threat to democracy as we still know it. My old friend Major Gil Down from Army Northern Command Intelligence near the old police barracks in Paddington was also hanging around during the riots, though clearly not in uniform! He was a good friend when I was called up some years earlier.

* * *

ALEC HARTLEY WAS A shopfitter who had done some work for my brother Nelson and so, as you do, I followed suit and engaged him to build and fit out my campus pharmacy. I also needed to obtain an approval number (5227D) from the Commonwealth Health Department as Alec's plans and equipment had to be in accordance with state Health Department regulations.

Unions did their level best to get a foothold with staff through the Miscellaneous Workers' Union. They were informed that people could think for themselves without a union boss doing it for them, which was a reasonable way of telling them to bugger off.

Pharmaceutical wholesalers had to be contacted to see if they would go guarantor for the business, with the rider that I purchased ninety-five per cent of my goods from them, which was a fair call. They would vary discounts on purchases and quickly remind you to pay up when dealing with a business which was starting out and every three months a set of figures such as income and purchases had to be provided. Later, year-on-year figures would also be scrutinised to see if they would continue their guarantee.

Then there were ancillary companies such as Kodak which were eager to come in. They had competition from others offering quicker developing and turnaround of processed films. But Kodak had the cameras and film so they had also to be massaged quite a bit to keep them onside. They were ruthless in demanding payment within thirty days.

Similar arrangements had to be set up with perfumery (Chanel, Fabergé, Tweed, 4711, and others). Revlon Cosmetics was the choice for the major brand offering over Helena Rubinstein, with Rimmel coming in later as a necessary cheaper brand and some sprinkling of Mary Quant, when available.

With all this to negotiate and payments to make, I had to open a bank account and offer Drug Houses of Australia as a reference as we did not have a home for them to get their sticky tentacles on, and strangle you if things went wrong. A guy called Gamble was the first person I met as manager, but no sooner had we established a relationship than he was transferred and another arrived. At one stage at least three died in a row, which was perplexing to say the least. The ABC would have claimed it was a cluster caused by aliens, even then as they moved to the Left politically.

So it was smart to get to know the bank treasurer and have a good relationship as they were more stable at a branch. The tellers were first responders for banking and change, so the odd exchange of good humour with them was worth a try. Remember, this was the side of the counter I was supposed to be working from!

With approval in principle to own the dispensary and retail outlet, the next step was to register the business name. If anyone had already done that, then some sort of challenge would go out to establish my bona-fides, with the approval in principle documentation. After about a month approval came through and the business name Campus Pharmacy, Shopping Centre, University of Queensland, St Lucia 4067, was now at the start of a long journey.

It was on 25 September 1970 that I became able to trade as Campus Pharmacy. There was no other in Queensland, so this was a history-making moment which had many doubting Thomases. For one thing, how would we manage during the lengthy university vacations and with only thirty-two teaching weeks a year? Sure, staff who were not on sabbatical leave would be around, but the pharmacy's location was as far as it could be from, for example, the post office and the J D Story Building, where administrative staff abound. On the positive side we had the refectories, and eventually a crepe outlet, which proved extremely popular until it was inexplicably closed.

As there was just one bank on campus and the small beginnings of a university credit union, the obvious choice was to go with the Commonwealth Bank of Australia. Like the pharmacy, it was located on a lower level, and that was a drawcard for staff and students seeking loans.

At the very beginning a clothing shop called Peter Shepherd opened between the pharmacy and the bank. It was very up to date with linked computerised register recording for all its stores around Australia. Trouble was, no student was going to buy clothes in between lectures, nor staff for that matter. Consequently their ambitious hopes fell by the way and after an odds-and-ends secondhand bookstore was mooted a bicycle shop eventually opened to some success. It is still there today, one level lower again and located near a dentist's surgery run by Dr Anne Fardoulys, which came much later, yet obviously successfully. Her mother's name was Poppy and they were of Greek origins.

The Campus Card and Gift Shop opened opposite the pharmacy, operated by Chadwick's, whose youngest son played tennis at BBC, a couple of years ahead of me. I did not warm to his loopy mannerisms on court, and no doubt he not to me.

Diagonally opposite the pharmacy was a hairdresser opened by a somewhat precious person followed by an openly gay male who was quite successful for many years. He cut Gillian's and my hair for a while and his diatribes about what he got up to in Fiji were fascinating to hear as he snipped away down the back of one's cranium. He was on a campus where freedom of speech was important and his sexual orientation was of no consequence.

It was sad when he told us he was selling up to a South American married couple, as he not surprisingly had caught HIV. This was the death knell, when the Grim Reaper splashed upon our screens. He told me he was going to Darwin to watch the sunsets with his mother, and that was where he passed away in a very horrible way.

No one in the precinct had an official lease, and most of them certainly had a backup business. Obviously the pharmacy and bank were the attractions for locating their retail outlets. The trouble was that the cost of setting up a pharmacy then and now is considerable. You need a long time to recover outgoings and make a profit when renting a place at Augustus Street, Toowong.

From a trading point of view opening the pharmacy in the latter part of the year, with an immediate need for cash flow, was by all accounts not the wisest business move on a campus devoid of students when they were on their mid-semester holidays. There was no summer semester then and no mass influx of overseas students (as distinct from now) to swell the campus in off-peak periods. But if I had not pushed for the opening of the pharmacy, no doubt someone else might well have done so and created a real quandary.

I could not have been aware at the time of opening that although there was a stubborn difficulty to get some sort of approved lease from the university, five years down the track, Griffith University, on the outskirts of Brisbane, was to open with 800 students and wanted to duplicate UQ by providing a shopping centre. UQ registrar Sam Rayner asked me if I would take it on as I already had the campus pharmacy. This was flattering, and some sort of paranoia set in that if I did not do what he had approached me to do it would be done by someone in Griffith's Nathan campus area.

Sam Rayner's assistant, John Topley, a tallish slow-spoken gentleman, had been appointed registrar at Griffith University.

For the opening of UQ Campus Pharmacy I had organised some opening sample bags, similar to those at Brisbane's annual royal show, which was where I had sat some final examinations in the wool pavilion! The bags were full of free goodies such as Kodak film, perfume phial samples and pamphlets for discounts on photo processing valid for a few months, hoping customers would hold on to their developing and printing until they came back from their Christmas holidays.

Photo processing offers were from Kodak and also an upcoming processor called Pacific Film. When either company representative came in, it was timely to hide the booklet so they could not see the number of dockets at the top, and also the collection pick-up bags. Pacific gave better discounts to me than Kodak. And a trading business is all about making profits wherever you can.

It soon became obvious that the pharmacy was too small during business peaks and so I approached the union for extra room beside the existing shop should it become available.

Student Travel Australia (STA) was already on campuses around Australia as a result of the demand for cheaper flights. Were there kickbacks? I didn't know, except from the rental all tenants paid to the union. Soon after my enquiries about expansion, STA moved up to street level, which was closer to eating places, and I would have happily exchanged location. The union was not interested, and explaining business principles from a tenant's point of view over the following years proved fruitless. After financial advisor Alf Pure left, his replacements were absolutely hopeless to the point that it was impossible to discuss rational business concerns.

The university was dancing to the tune that if all was quiet on the western front (the union) it would stay out of it as long as it had a rough idea of what was going on. Every student was charged a compulsory annual union fee at a time when HECS fees were still a little way off. Some of the fee went to the sports union, and to affiliation with the National Union of Students (NUS), which was ultra-left in politics. It was the NUS that had pushed for the friendly society pharmacy and had missed out until a new opportunity arose. It licked its wounds by opening a grocery store down below the pharmacy, which lost money and rotting stock through poor management and a cash-only register. It had cheaper vegies on Saturdays, which just sat on the makeshift shelves as few people bothered to shop there. The dude who was always hustling me set this shop up as some testament to his socialist intent, rather than a cooperative understanding of when and where to do something that is fiscally prudent. And they were not required to pay any rent nor show even a token amount for the part that was occupied as other tenants did. It was touted as a pop-up shop benefiting membership of the NUS.

The NUS did much to destroy the concept of a fair go for students by being like a cancerous growth on university campuses around Australia. It held annual and biannual conferences interstate, hosted by a different state each year, and attended by burgeoning numbers of delegates, all expenses paid courtesy of the compulsory union fees sealed by university approval.

The NUS appeared on student union voting papers, although voting was never compulsory. It had manifested itself as having representatives from each faculty on campus but increasing apathy or vote rigging determined the winners. Each year it elected a new president, whose politics may well be completely opposite to those of the previous president and union council.

* * *

ONE DAY, AT THE suggestion of the then general manager of DHA, Brisbane, I took a significant risk and flew to Sydney to look at Australia's only other campus pharmacy, leaving final year girl Darrien to hold the fort. I was met at Sydney Airport by DHA's New South Wales general manager and driven to the University of Sydney where a pharmacy had just opened.

It was located near the university bookshop and sort of privately owned, or in talks with a friendly society's pharmacy group about a change of ownership. This meant less profit for DHA if it went ahead with the existing supply chain.

I was able to gain some insights at my own expense of flying to Sydney, there and back in one day. Darrien coped well and no inspectors had come in. Later she joined me at the Campus Pharmacy when it opened. It was there I signed off this future pharmacist, barrister and I believe judge. We also went to her wedding a few years later.

Did I wish to be cooped up in a dispensary, which was modern but small, looking out the rear window towards the river and endless expanses of green dotted with palm trees? I did not. It was restrictive in size, the profession was restrictive and there was no knowing where this would all finish up. By now my years at BBC were far behind in my thoughts, the Vietnam War was still on and providing for my wife was important as she adjusted in different ways to the drudgery of routine. It was always difficult in the heat of summer and seasonal decline in sales made it always impossible to accept and budget for the downturn.

They were different times to now when generations of people have never known inflation, nor anything but freedom fought for by the generations before them.

We eventually got the extension to the pharmacy (plus pro rata rent) and I did the fixtures alterations on a budget, leaving the floor as it was with the union kindly providing cleaning and floor buffing and polishing for me. Cleaning stopped short of actually touching drugs and only cleaning in my presence. We were all paranoid that something would go wrong and reach the *Courier Mail*. Adverse publicity of drugs being stolen on campus was too much for the university to contemplate.

I once disposed of some expired drugs on a Friday morning and some deplorable person rummaged through the large industrial bin and spilt the drugs on the bitumen of the car park. The bin was not emptied as usual and so this state of affairs existed all weekend. As a result, the proverbial hit the fan accompanied by please explains and strong words from the university. In its self-protective arrogant and ignorant response it referred to people working in their ivory tower. It blew over, though I did not need that, and I started sending later drugs back to the wholesaler for disposal.

With almost a year's figures to show, and with our accountants being Peat Marwick Mitchell (formerly KPMG), who were engaged at a reduced fee because of Gillian's Uncle Chris being a partner in London and Paris, I made an appointment with the Commonwealth Bank to sound them out about a housing loan – how much they would lend and what they would require in securities for their regional manager's approval?

There were limits for approvals that a branch manager could 'afford'. Lending then was only to the primary earner. Even if the wife was earning it made no difference. From my perspective, this is ridiculous. In case of the death of the primary earner, the surviving spouse should ensure they at least have a credit card in their name, otherwise the banks shut the doors on you for a few months to sort things out.

So without a lease, only a couple of years of trading figures and credit extended by DHA, I sat with Gillian in the bank manager's office at the CBA's UQ branch and said we had found a unit near Macquarie Street, St Lucia. The REIQ contract was cheekily presented. The block where the unit was situated was ahead of its time and is still there today where the Dutton Park Ferry once called. It was only two bedrooms and one bathroom, with glimpses of the Brisbane River from a pleasant balcony. It had only recently been completed and located in a cul-de-sac lined with lovely spreading trees. The units mostly faced the river and on one side was the spacious Guyatt Park, which now is the docking point for the CityCat ferries.

If successful, our loan application would give us our very first home together at the block known as Trenton. Without, as yet, any children, the cost was the princely sum of $19,000 before extras such as legal fees, stamp duty, bank and loan lodgement fees, insurance protection for the loan and registration with the council. There were no doubt many more.

It took a few days to approve and we put the unit under contract with a fourteen-day finance clause, subject to pest and building inspection. Banks are very profitable as a share investment from all of the above income, though we did not have the money to buy shares. They make huge profits lending other people's money. I detest them.

With the benefit of hindsight, the worst thing we did was to not keep the unit. Just imagine what it would be worth today. It would have been a good long-term investment, but it was not to be. When investing, Australians' love of owning their own house was then paramount, whereas owning a unit was regarded differently then, and now more so; on and off, the property mood swings come and go. The major asset we had (or rather I had because of the then-strict ownership rules) was Campus Pharmacy.

A popular gregarious chap called Terry White, along with wife Rhonda, popped in one day on his way to the crêperie and had a chat. He became a member of the state government, later leaving to create the Australia-wide chain of pharmacies that merged with Chemmart in 2016. Two years later the White family sold their remaining stake in TerryWhite Chemmart to Australasian healthcare group EBOS for $50 million. He had started in Redcliffe and the link here is the matter of multiple ownerships.

Our loan was approved and we had succeeded in getting on the property ladder at a time when interest rates were much higher than the so-called doom and gloom ones of today. Our hope was that inflation would clear the debt over twenty-five years. If we could pay off more, well and good, everyone had to stay healthy, and Bob's your uncle. No holidays, no guaranteed income, as in a public service job, and life was sweet.

* * *

I HATE THE EXPRESSION that a woman falls pregnant. We did wish to have a child and thus truly consummate what marriage actually entails. And it takes two to tango. So it was that Trenton, by the Brisbane River, became the home of our first born, Sara Jane Hunt-Sharp. Sara was born at Brisbane's Mater Hospital after an extremely long and harrowing time for her and Gillian. I was told to go home and come back later as labour pains continued in the maternity ward. However as I reached the end of a corridor on my way out, Nelson suddenly appeared to offer his support. I remember someone saying that I was as white as a sheet.

This was in the days when nurses and nuns (in this case) did not allow a husband near his wife during labour as holding hands or assisting in the birth was forbidden. The husband waited for the baby to be brought out to him and eventually you would see your wife and hope all were safe and well. Checking little fingers and toes would always be the strange way of eventually looking at our little girl, who clearly had been subject to enormous contractions before Dr O'Connor decided on a caesarean.

Coincidently he was an old boy from BBC and delivered our son, Peter Jesse Hunt-Sharp, two years later at the Royal Brisbane Hospital where my university mate John Cox was a registrar doing midwifery. He had known Gillian well and stopped by at Trenton on his way to lectures at UQ. He went on to do paediatrics and now lives in Toowoomba. His wife is Scottish. His father had been a pharmacist in Gympie and had been wealthy with a property at Alexandra Headland, on the Sunshine Coast just north of Mooloolaba. We are diametrically opposites, with me from a poor background and he from a wealthy one. So be it! He was a boarder at Anglican Grammar School, 'Churchie', at the same time as Eric Barton. This was when I was at BBC.

* * *

It was some years before I received a dutifully sealed lease as an addendum with the university seal to boot, attached to the union lease agreement. Alan Thorpe only charged for the final documentation as otherwise, he said, fees would have been astronomical. He was an RAAF reserve lawyer in an honorary capacity of sorts.

No one teaches negotiation skills for business matters, and it is a case of putting the right suggestion forward at the right time. It also helps to take advantage of any situation that arises. That is the secret to negotiation. No one in my family really knew what stress this put me under, and the need for stress releases came with a chance to gain some advantage.

When one gets given a good decision it never ends there because ultimately one has to answer to conscience and realise, if it comes to money and success, only the operator knows what it is all about. I have never signed a tax return without a disclaimer for absolving the accountants from liability. They can only advise on what you present, and it is cheaper to present everything possible for fine tuning and presentation to the ATO, which we still do through our present accountants.

Fortunately, as time went by, Gillian was willing and keen to take an interest in pharmacy on the retail side and also in seeking the best discounts available on dispensary purchases. She had worked at a child minding clinic that was then at Indooroopilly Shopping Centre. In charge was Sister Turner, a lovely person who had trained at the old private hospital attached to Brisbane's St John's Cathedral. Her son, Ian, who became a friend, was a bursar at Gatton College before it was swallowed up by UQ to supplement the university's veterinary farm at Moggill, which was already attached to its veterinary school. It had its own dispensary and very occasionally I made contact as it was eventually required to employ a registered pharmacist.

By 1970 I had successfully opened the Campus Pharmacy, the first of its kind, and extended it by fifty per cent and now had a growing business. The shopping arcade where I was located was doing pretty well and I set in train a progress association, mainly for tenants' rights. I had also established a good working relationship with the university's health service medicos, with some early heads of the Medical Centre being rather left of centre.

I was being pushed to make a decision on opening a pharmacy at Griffith University and there was something niggling me to find a way of being less restrictive on a day-to-day basis if I went ahead. Explorative suggestions were under way as to what was going to be there – I was told a part-time visiting GP (Gina Smith) and a psychologist but, apart from the National Australia Bank and a nearby refectory, nothing else. They would have loved a post office as well, but Australia Post indicated it was not economical for them. The problem in dealing with administrative officials and bureaucrats was their ever-present lack of retailing knowledge. They wanted a private service provider to wear a loss for them so they could say to future students and staff, 'Look what we have at Griffith University, at the Nathan campus; it is just as good as UQ'.

This was the time for a new university to compete for student enrolments which would be largely subsidised by the Commonwealth government. Its profit depended on student numbers and so it introduced different courses that placed much emphasis on environmental studies. While this began to seem like a lefty's paradise, it also coincided with lower entrance requirements for students. It built state and Commonwealth-funded student accommodation, provided a gymnasium of sorts and had pleasant landscaped grounds in the bush on a hill at Mt Gravatt (Nathan). Student colleges at UQ were based on the British model of campus colleges, which, for me, was far better than Griffith's.

I was privileged to see its first logo, which I thought was good, although a small fortune was budgeted to achieve what you see today. Why a logo? Well, it identified a university in some way but was really a marketing idea imported from America.

Needless to say, with the figurative success under way at UQ, I had a definite desire to expand and sold the concept to myself and to a cautious Gillian. We enquired about non-official post offices and found that Australia Post was very receptive to us opening one provided we were of good character. So here we were taking on another bureaucracy to help the Griffith one. We were perhaps not as stupid as we seemed. Apart from selling postage stamps, which we knew nothing about, non-official post offices came with a Commonwealth Bank outlet. Imagine the furore from the NAB, which had gone on to the campus with sole rights for banking, and rightly so. But it was also the bank for the university, as distinct from the CBA then being in that position at UQ.

The ANZ bank arrived at UQ, it is said, because the then vice chancellor was put out by having to walk and wait for far too long at the CBA and said, 'I want another bank on campus' (it already had a post office and the CBA branch). Bingo! Room was promptly found at the university staff club. Like falling dominoes, NAB followed and automatic tellers soon abounded.

When we were trading at UQ, the Coca Cola sales at the refectories were the largest in Australia. It was the largest seller, which makes sense in a student demographic. Even with that and with all the rental incomes from tenants the university Student Union still managed to make a loss. Even the student fees went up in smoke, which necessitated rises to the poor enrolled students.

During the 1982 Commonwealth Games products bearing the Australian coat of arms were the only things we were licensed to sell, with royalties going to the university. The university logo appeared much later and was never used to my knowledge during the Commonwealth Games memorabilia sales. We found the Games logo to be the most acceptable for athletes from the Commonwealth when buying souvenirs. There was no way of knowing this when Gillian was placing vast orders for memorabilia.

In those days student prescriptions were largely subsidised on production of their student health care card number. This subsidised PBS scripts. Often this would be produced after dispensing as a general PBS, which meant doing it all over again. We soon made it mandatory to ask if they had a card to avoid having to dispense it twice. In the beginning script typing was a cumbersome process of using the trusty Remington or Olivetti typewriter and feeding in carbon impregnated repeat scripts. Computers were still yet to appear.

We had a very good rapport with staff and students, and as the numbers grew with enrolments, new buildings blossomed thanks to a Commonwealth cash splash.

As the Campus Pharmacy sales grew, so did our capacity to borrow. After several years we had a duly signed lease which I swear aged me considerably to obtain. Sara was around two years of age and Gillian put her in a wading pool at the back where the garages were to splash around with much delight. Around this time we had decided to have a second child, and wouldn't it be nice if conception resulted in giving us a boy. People preferred mostly to find out the sex of the child at birth.

Peter Jesse Hunt-Sharp came into this world at the RBH. He had the umbilical cord wrapped around his neck, so when contractions started there was a problem in trying to save him from exhaustion. Sara had been a face presentation, and in both cases a caesarean was needed. This time labour was not prolonged by a Catholic desire for a natural birth and before too long we had two siblings living with us at our single bedroom unit at Trenton.

I remember an occasion when Gillian was heavily pregnant with Peter and trying to rock Sara to sleep on the balcony when an Indian history professor and customer we knew called out to Gillian 'Is the Messiah born yet?' That Indian couple used to order pharmaceutical-grade olive oil in gallon cans from the pharmacy, for bathing. Their hair glimmered in the moonlight as they caught the ferry to South Brisbane. It was a time when a couple of other lecturers and friends Gillian had made from child minding would pop in for a drink. She had become very friendly with a married couple who lived in a front unit, almost on the river. 'Mrs P' and Gillian would chat over a wine and a cigarette on the balcony. Mr Perkins had been the architect to Woolworths and had designed its store at Toowong, which is now a large and empty valuable block ready for development.

With a small unit, it was time to return to the CBA at UQ and ask if we could trade the unit in for a house at Bowaga Street, Indooroopilly, and whether they would lend sufficient money for the purchase and to complete the sale. We would have to sell the unit, which later we both regretted, but we did not have the capacity to own the two, let alone the possibility of two pharmacies.

We bought the house and the CBA now had a second mortgage over our property and DHA over our business. If anything went wrong, the first bite of the cherry is always the tax office followed by the bank.

* * *

IN THE BREAKFAST ROOM at Bowaga Street there was a window seat where my father sat and counted Gillian's contractions that March night. I was in contact with the obstetrician, Dan O'Connor, who eventually said Gillian should go to the RBWH where she was admitted by a fussy matron.

On the way we stopped at the Regatta pub drive-in and bought a half bottle of Gordons gin. No need to hurry, besides, hasten slowly can be a good idea at times. Everything went well in the end and Peter emerged from the C-Section. The duty registrar John Cox got to see him first and told Gillian and I all was okay.

The Bowaga Street house was ready and waiting for the new baby. It had three bedrooms and a chandelier over the internal staircase leading to a rumpus-cum-garage underneath. It was not architect designed so there were obvious failings, but it was home. The driveway was steep and sloped downwards with water always flowing over rusty grates which were not large enough to capture heavier downpours.

Monica flew over briefly from the UK as she had said she had to return to be at Angela's for the christening of Angela's daughter Rachael. This was a bit of a kick in the stomach for Gillian with two young children and me at a demanding professional workplace. But all was not lost because Aunty Annie offered her only daughter to babysit and do general cleaning in the house. She was so inadequate to the task that it was like having a third child.

Peter was born on 13 March 1974. In the January before, Brisbane had three weeks of record rainfall. The Brisbane River broke its banks leaving the Regatta pub and Coronation Drive well and truly flooded. That bloody drain in our garage had been continually scraped out by Gillian lifting the heavy grates over it. Then she dropped a grate on her big toe, fracturing it into little pieces. Almost fainting with blood and rain streaming down in sheets, she made her way upstairs where Sara comforted her and helped her phone the Pharmacy.

I rang the GP on duty at the service, a Doctor Bottcher, and asked if he could see Gillian as all roads were closed by the heavy rain, and he agreed. They had some sterile treating ability, which was useful at that time. Everything was shutting so I sent the shop girl home and took off to Bowaga Street to get Gillian. Water was streaming across the end of Lambert Road and although I hit it with some force, the waters parted and I motored the relatively short distance to Gillian, who was pregnant with Peter and bleeding with excruciating pain from her fractured big toe.

On the way back to the health service I was stopped by a police car and told not to proceed. With some persuasion and curious looks they gave us a police escort back to the university entrance.

Meanwhile, my parents were already panicking as the water was rising from a blocked stormwater drain at the end of Munro Street where the tennis court was. They watched as the floods quickly rose several metres until it lapped their floorboards. As if in a war zone, a bunch of Vietnam veterans and others got to 50 Warren Street where they raised all the furniture in case the water came any further and higher. They did a hell of a good job, there and elsewhere.

My parents were eventually evacuated and they stayed with us. This was a time when the milkman still called at the house and it is sad that this service is no more. As our milkman was flood bound, neighbours suggested that he drive to nearby St Peter's Lutheran College where he could give out milk from his van to those who called. Ours was brought down the hill by those same kindly neighbours, when he was unable to deliver. People were helping each other in a time of necessity, which was great. Our milk order had increased at a time when it was rationed because of the flood.

Somehow people survive and so they can move on. The sour stench of the mud remains fixed in the olfactory area of the brain, as something difficult to describe.

While at Bowaga Street, we acquired a beautiful labrador dog complete with papers showing his pedigree name as Charamala Dream Time. We decided to call him Time. He grew with the children from a puppy, and Sara and Peter adored him as much as he adored them. This was the first time Gillian had had a pet dog. He used to sit by the front door but was not much of a watchdog as he wagged his tail at most people and barked rarely.

* * *

Our next move was to a house in Pylara Street, Fig Tree Pocket, which cost around $115,000 and sat on a 2.5-acre block.

Although not a modern house, it was certainly to become one which was the most popular with the family. We had chooks, a little pond and a dirt roadway entrance down the property. After building the chook run, we bought a horse with the help of my father. He was a small speckled grey and quite bad tempered. There was an existing pool with some old landscaping around the fringes. The adjoining land towards the east consisted of three easements to properties at the back, which brought them close to the Fig Tree Pocket Pony Club. Another easement which went down to those properties had an interesting history.

By now my love of tennis had really taken over and I decided to install a tennis court beyond the pool. I hired a fellow from Seventeen Mile Rocks, who quoted for a retaining wall which was quick and free standing. After a while of hitting against the wall for practice, I was sure the wall, which was in sections, had moved on its axis. It looked like the Berlin Wall panels and similar constructions. It was probably where this sheep farmer or his connections in South Australia had got the idea. The problem was that it was not a free-standing wall, with no drainage or compacted soil behind, and he lacked the engineering skills to realise that. It needed drainage to prevent water pooling and causing the ultimate frightening experience of having the whole thing fall after heavy rain.

This left the pool in a precarious state with all that weight of water bearing down on it. Sara was with me when we walked down our private dirt road one morning before work and school.

As we looked on, the entire wall collapsed with a resounding noise one section at a time. It was a heart-breaking moment that I took years to get over. Repairs were done by an engineer friend who also became an expert witness in court when I claimed damages. I engaged MFC (Minter Ellison) who provided a contractual lawyer, and a barrister from a well-known family.

At the time, I was coaching the daughter of Dr David Pincus, who had practised near my brother's pharmacy in Stafford and the opportunity arose to ask if I could speak to his well-known barrister brother about the case. This was during the presentation proceedings to research as much as possible.

Some people call themselves coaches in various sports simply by deciding to be one. Tennis was one of the sports to get that sorted out early on with various examinations and coaching courses extending over a couple of years. I had completed these at the Milton Tennis Centre with Mal Murphy, who was a fine coach and old school in all respects. Tennis was firing at Milton and Mal had billeted a ranked player from Florida, USA, whom I mentored and guided through nutritional aspects. I remember being called from courtside by Gillian to say that the results of the court battle had come in. I had won part, but did not get damages, and faced the possibility of paying the other party's legal costs. It was a real gut-wrenching moment!

Getting a loan to repair the court and surreptitiously also pay for some of my legal costs came at a time when the CBA was right behind tennis in Queensland. At major events it had large marquees for honoured guests, and wining and dining them like a miniature Wimbledon. They loaned me more money and

I became quite friendly with the manager who had a strong resemblance to Mr Bean. I was wined and dined at head office in the city. I was fascinated by driving onto a circular concrete area which rotated your car towards a vacant car park. The state manager spoke highly of Ballandean Wines and a variety of them was served to us over that Friday lunch.

Was Pylara Street jinxed? Or was it just time to have some more of the bad luck life can dish out? I soon learnt the answer when a neighbour served a deposition upon us to be given access to the other dirt road. Why would he do that? That was what I decided to find out by engaging a lawyer from a Toowong legal firm. We remain friends today. He was also a tennis enthusiast and was friendly with Wimbledon title winner Ken Fletcher. He was later divorced and lost his house and tennis court as a consequence. He was also friendly with tennis enthusiast and writer Hugh Lunn, a close friend of Fletcher.

It was on New Year's Eve that the neighbour came to our house and offered cash to allow his proposed real estate venture, saying to Gillian that we could probably use the money. All we had to do was sign a document to that affect. What would neighbours further down their easement think?

After a while the domino effect set in as Paul Keating raised interest rates, which eventually led to many bankruptcies. Keating, a pig farmer-cum-antique clock collector, was the epitome of a pseudo-Labor leader, and this was a turning point for all businesses and home owners in 'the banana state'.

PLAYING GAMES

We had now established the Campus Shoppe at Griffith University with a lease directly with the university unlike the one at UQ. It had a student representative council (SRC) to let the eighteen-year-olds practice their politics and with Environmental and Asian studies then forefront in academia, the rest was pretty obvious.

Student unions then and now produce political leaders, mostly of Labor persuasion. Churning out a degree for the sake of it became the mantra and when the Commonwealth Games came round they were in the mood to become retailers of their own merchandise as distinct from the official games merchandise. (CGM).

With the CGM the royalties went straight to the foundation, at time of purchase. Whereas the university produced its own logo-branded t-shirts and loads of windcheaters, which they felt a reasonable idea as those with money were coming from colder climates, even though it was September and pleasant in Brisbane.

When a government or semi-government authority, and I specifically refer to universities, makes a loss it is the taxpayer who wears a discretionary loss which is buried in many layers of bureaucracy.

Having learned that careful wording is important in a lease, we had a clause, taken from the UQ lease, which stated (roughly) we had exclusive rights to provide all retail sales of all goods and services normally stocked by a pharmacy, newsagency, post office, gift shop and dry cleaning. The pharmacy was separately designated as a dispensary, which was a part-time one with its own PBS approval number. So, like a part-time health service, I would match their hours. Gillian ran the post office and retail buying and we moved stock from one to the other. For the Commonwealth Games we used the billiard table at Pylara Street to check and sort sizes and price the multitude of t-shirts.

It would take a separate book to discover and achieve the entire goings on for the process leading up to the 1982 Commonwealth Games. I was fortunate in setting up all the retail outlets to have the UQ experience behind me and when it got out that we had exclusive rights on campus to sell memorabilia, our telephone rang hot. Instead of being sensible negotiators the university should have gone through us for sales of its merchandise.

I had some fiery conversations with a Griffith University Scottish bully, along the lines of what he intended to do. He argued he had experience from the Edinburgh Commonwealth Games and I matched him saying I had already seen that set up, where the university was an entirely different demographic. He had no definitive job description and I quietly regarded him as a jumped-up warehouse manager, who was difficult to understand due to his inflective vocabulary. He was told to honour the agreement, and raise this with registrar Topley, or it was game over after the games as they needed me more than I needed them in the services we provided. The bluff paid off. Though the task ahead was great with no figures available from the past.

Cartons of t-shirts with the simple but good logo arrived at Pylara Street, where Gillian checked them off. She found numerous errors of short sending, as various deliveries arrived over weeks. Would there be enough or had we underestimated, and where or how would we fund this completely new business on top of the major one at Campus Pharmacy?

It was two weeks of retailing daily from 8.30 am until around 7.30 pm. The university went to ground so far as assisting us and telling athletes where they could find us. So we produced pamphlets which added expense and myself or our staff dropped them around dining halls and lounges on the campus.

The Mt Gravatt shop must have sold some product but we would never know what. Besides, they were concentrating on ticket sales to swell the coffers of the Commonwealth Games Foundation. We were also asked by the games' organisers if we would provide a coffee shop at Mt Gravatt Teachers' College Roundhouse. This was relatively easily done as everything was provided by a coffee supplier, and it was then that we discovered how profitable cappuccinos can be.

We were fortunate that there were no other retail outlets close by and that the foundation took over the campus, with boom gates at the winding bitumen entrance. We had highest level security passes, which were coloured and probably barcoded and had to be produced every time we drove in. It was easy to have the pass on a lanyard and take it off when parking out the back behind the pharmacy next to the NAB manager's allocated space.

There was also an ambulance designated parking area, which was used by the chauffeured Rolls Royce from Government House which brought Queen Elizabeth II to visit the athletes' centre.

The campus was in a security lockdown, and all deliveries were screened, which was a good reason to check orders and redeliver them when we travelled to work. Some people took it upon themselves to send stock postage paid, and on one occasion we had a security alert when the bomb checkers arrived with a parcel which we had not been expecting. A resonance occurred as they passed their machine over the parcel and the needle on their monitor was spiking. Instead of bringing in the bomb squad, they asked us to open it slowly as they thought it would be okay. It turned out to be magnetic CD sporting tapes, which I put to one side as it was so ridiculous. After the games the owners had fourteen days to pick them up, or they would be dumped. They were dumped.

DEEKS' WINNING POTION

A shortish young wiry fellow popped into the pharmacy before things got under way for the marathon and asked if we could secure an Abbott pharmaceutical product.

He had tried all over the place. As a biochemist he was aware of clinical trial papers suggesting to him that the product would be worth trying for his event. It may well have been Ensure powder which was relatively new to Australia.

Australia was on its feet when Rob de Castella – known throughout the running community as 'Deeks' – held off the African challengers to win the games marathon. He told me later that without that electrolyte supplement he would have never done it.

The marathon followed a blue line which passed through the UQ campus and it gave everybody an understanding of how long a distance a marathon is. We met many interesting athletes from countries throughout the Commonwealth. One fellow, who won the gold medal for pistol shooting, left it on our counter and popped in a day or so later to pick it up. He was with special forces in London, but that was as far as he was forthcoming. He left early, not bothering with the closing ceremony as he had his work to go back to.

What really struck me was the hospitality of the British team who invited me a few times for drinks in their team headquarters on the Griffith campus. They had plenty of gin (Gordons) and poured large measures. Their chef de mission was a woman who almost bought a huge specially engraved punchbowl we had on consignment from McKinney's in Toowoomba. She decided against the purchase as it would be a hassle on the plane, even though McKinney's offered to package and send it. What a shame it is not in the archives as a museum piece back in England, now as I write.

We managed to trade many stick pins for our Australian ones and stocked stacks of logo ones and others from those that made general Australiana stick pins. Someone decided to frame them and offer them for sale, but there were only a few who bought them, one being Griffith University. Somewhere it will still be hanging on a wall in perhaps their sports pavilion.

The more expensive the item, the less likely was an athlete to make a purchase. Things such as handkerchiefs or epaulettes were hard to sell; though neckties bearing the logo backed with blue in silk were quite popular. In a white box, they made a perfect gift for Dad back home. Water bottles were of occasional interest, and this prompted me to print my own for Campus Pharmacy UQ as a promotional item, for the UQ Rugby Club and later for the Wests Rugby Club at Toowong.

But the coup de grace for me was to negotiate the flag and his cap crown from the chauffeur of the Queen's Rolls Royce when he was parked waiting for her. He said she had gone for a stroll to look at the beautiful flora and fauna around the campus close to our shop; so I walked off and the Queen and I came face to face and neither of us spoke; though I am sure she was relieved to see the lanyard I was wearing as her lady-in-waiting quickly rushed up to be with her.

The Queen, wearing a pale floral dress, was complete with hat, handbag and gloves. She was also feeling the heat of September and probably wished to get back to the air conditioning of the Rolls. (With the Queen's flag, the driver always kept a spare in the reddish Rolls glove box.)

We found the best seller to be a white collarless t-shirt with the logo smack in the middle. Other shades and colours were available but when ordering from the Gold Coast supplier, Gillian stipulated them to be mostly white.

None of the logo shirts and assorted items could be purchased on consignment. They arrived in various sizes, which had to be checked off and then folded on that useful billiard table downstairs which looked out over the pool and the eventually doomed tennis court. We created an area in the shop for a folded t-shirt display, with a sign to where various sizes could be flicked trough on a borrowed clothes display on wheels.

The smart arse with all the Griffith University windcheaters, was given an opportunity to sell through us when he found he was not managing to sell many at his little booth up wherever it was. Learning from our experience by then we welcomed him only on the condition they were on consignment. After the games they had cartons of memorabilia which they eventually could not sell and as far as I know they donated them to some third world country.

The moral to the story is that academia should never tamper

or think they can be retailers unless they have a captive market such as through the University Press where mandatory course books were required. Lab coats always sold well at UQ, as did dissection kits. But the market is always changing and the biggest revenue as a tax against students comes from the parking charges. Affiliation fees to various clubs are separate to the union and sports union.

We had secured a loan against my parents' property, much to the chagrin of Nelson and Narelle for their own personal reasons. It was a time when Treasurer Keating was presiding over a twenty-one per cent interest rate, which was what we had to pay on a six-month temporary overdraft. Everything would have started tumbling down if we did not repay that amount, not that my parents cared.

On the last day of competition, Gillian, who was banking at the NAB each day, checked the overdraft balance and found it had just been paid out. It took 20 000 shirts, with a few left over, to clear that borrowing and exit the mortgage against Warren Street. So in about ten days of trading until about 7.0 pm each day with two young children, we had a turnover of at least $250 000 in 1982 Commonwealth Games memorabilia.

With little profit, we counted it as an experience and, with all the bad luck at Pylara Street, we eventually sold to a person who displayed a rather impolite manner as Gillian was still scrubbing the floors as settlement went through.

* * *

THERE WAS AN EERIE silence after the games ended, particularly as the university semesters had been changed and there was no real trade until the next February in the campus shop at Griffith. We had owned the Griffith University post office adjacent to the campus shop-cum-newsagent and part-time dispensary. Now it was time to move on or the result would be financially disastrous.

Gillian managed the most profitable part which was the post office. This was so busy it required a staff member, named Shirley, who was an experienced non-official post office worker. But it had no goodwill, and when the GPO decided the time was right, they put in an official one.

Shirley had sometimes rented the little cottage we had bought at Marcoola for around $18 000 from tennis coach Mal Murphy. That was an exceptional period for our children and every long weekend, Easter or Christmas we would be there within walking distance of Marcoola Beach, which had its own surf lifesaving club.

We got to know the locals including one or two bums. It was here that Sara and Peter joined the Nippers at Marcoola Surf Club, which was something they loved. I took them fishing every chance I could. The golden labrador Time was with us and he enjoyed the beach. He eventually died at Pylara Street in Gillian's arms.

It was also a time when I had a Rover 3.5 litre sedan car which was notoriously unreliable. Eventually smoke came from the seat belt area when I was driving a young local lad who trawled for sea sand worms using meat on a string for bait and who had rescued Pete from the treacherous tidal mouth of the Mooloolah River. He asked quietly if this was normal. I traded it in on a large Ford Cartier LTD. And locked in some cash for a lease balloon payment. Gillian still has some leather Cartier products which came with the LTD. It was a bulky limited edition that just fitted into the driveway at the little lean-to at the side of the beach house.

STEEP LEARNING CURVE

After the games, we were liquidity low and starting to bleed money with the Griffith campus shop. The only real goodwill value was the approval number, which was not by acquisition but by establishing the part-time dispensary in the first place.

We put the word out via a person at Fauldings that it was for sale, including everything pertaining to the lease which was the other saleable asset. When we established the business the university insisted we pay for the installation of the tiled ceiling, which was to prove its undoing. In the end we sold it to the wife of a lawyer, who was a pharmacist with a father who was a newsagent. The sale went through for a bargain basement price and we used the proceeds to pay down overall debt, personal and business.

Gillian was particularly good at seeing the picture from the outside, while I struggled with the intensity of dispensing. After they had purchased the pharmacy (which operated part-time, suiting the woman with young children), the university started trying some funny things concerning the rental and came a gutser. With the help of her lawyer husband she transferred the approval number to a business opening in Sunnybank, which was in the prescribed limit of the Act in respect of approval numbers.

They then proceeded to set up a new business and did very well, taking many fixtures with them, including the dangerous-drugs safe. As a result of the conflict, the university has never had a pharmacy since. All this did not happen without a legal battle, which I was very aware to stay well clear of except to assist where possible with general matters. Griffith University began flexing its muscles and argued that the approval number should remain with its campus as that was where it was originally assigned to and it should not be transferred elsewhere. To the owner's relief the tribunal found in favour of the respondents.

* * *

WE HAD AN ACCOUNTANT who wisely said never sell the Campus Pharmacy as it was by far the finest asset we had. Now with considerable dislike for confinement, my mobility outside the confines of Campus Pharmacy, UQ, ended with the return to full-time managing of Campus Pharmacy, which had been run down by a series of full-time and part-time pharmacists. I kept a part-time pharmacist on for Friday afternoons and demonstrators at the pharmacy school were usually happy for the extra cash and escape from academia that this provided.

I discovered one of these pharmacists, Margaret Robinson (better known as Margot), often used to have a seafood fest with some friends. She was instrumental in introducing counselling as a subject for pharmacy students. It made me chuckle when I sprung them one day.

Another honours graduate, Ros Brand, now at the Wesley Hospital, would do a few Fridays as well.

There was an increased suppressed vigour now I was back on my own again as I had to trade down a lot of debt caused by the interest rate increases and sheer arseholes who will take advantage of you any time they can. We had a negatively geared house at Payne Street, Auchenflower, which we sold. We loved that tiny cottage. Another property, along Milton Road, was never going to be any good so goodness knows why I was talked into it. We had the luxury of the Flindersia Street house at Marcoola which we were renting out and ferals were trashing it. One fridge had been completely spray painted and taken away to another property.

I remember walking into the CBA at UQ and being told the rates were now at sixteen per cent for negative gearing. Gillian was worried, so we eventually sold the lot, but withholding a block of land in my name at Munro Street, upon which most of the tennis court fitted. The adjoining allotment was in Narelle's name and Nelson had declined. We had paid only $350 when my parents needed extra cash as a help out when they built at the front. I had bought this before going to the UK.

Some years later, when we again needed cash, we sold the two lots at the rear for $240 000 but getting that sale finalised on the veranda at Toowong was sheer torture as my sister was a real problem. Patrick stayed the distance and eventually the contract was signed by Narelle as well. She didn't need the money, but we would have found it useful. When we used the tennis court with friends all she could do was threaten us not to go on her land. She became friends with a UQ professor and they made a lot of money with her then architect husband Stewart.

I really can't detail everything that happened at the time, whether it was my poor management or choosing the wrong profession or lack of confidence in the chosen profession. But rather than sit and rely upon self-pity and dodgy outcomes it was time to actually focus. I was a Level 3 professional tennis coach, a pharmacist, the youngest JP ever, and many years later Gillian discovered I was entitled to a couple of medals from the Vietnam era.

None of these would ever pay the bills and there was an asset sale that began with getting rid of the beloved lifestyle at Marcoola and negatively geared properties. There were charlatans encountered along the way, but I won't honour them by mentioning their names, but I know who they are.

As the saying goes, 'When one door closes, another opens'. There was to be a revamp of the UQ union buildings and expressions of interest were sought for a new administration building. This provided an opportunity to move the CBA, the union's bank, to Circular Road level. When we had first opened down at the subterranean level, the Schonell Theatre was finally completed. It is a fine bit of architecture, and thousands of people enjoyed theatre and cinema there. Barrister Robert Wensley, a sometime union president and senate member guided this project. On the theatrical side, a chap from Toowoomba, the renowned actor Geoffrey Rush, made his stage debut there before later winning an Oscar. We provided samples of perfume and the like for various evening performances when something special was on.

A financial controller, a diligent equivalent to Alf Pure, was advising everybody and seeking opinions on where they would like to be located. The rider to all that was that the student union council had the final say. After much lobbying and juggling, and at the risk of making enemies, we secured the prime spot for the location of Campus Pharmacy. No one knew what I went through, including a battle over the bike shop which was happy around the back of the new arcade and near the revamped refectory. There were new coffee outlets and eventually a fine wood-fired pizza kiosk was built near the Schonell. It was super popular all the time and also opened on Saturdays, or when a Schonell function was on. It was a real success story.

Our location was good but there had to be a refit, which was not as easy as it sounds. We had to maximise the retail area and allow for the dispensary. So for the second time at UQ, and third overall when Griffith University was included, I contacted Hartley Shopfitters who drew up plans for the new location. It was a traditional step-up dispensary, with a back door entrance to other shops such as a hairdresser and a menswear shop (later an outlet for UQ memorabilia). Another shop provided photocopying but that was short lived as the union decided to instal its own coin-operated machine for anytime use provided the entrance to the building was open. Outside there was provided a bank of microwaves for students to heat up their meals brought with them from wherever they were billeted at the time.

Sales increased dramatically in all respects, including photo processing, and by now we had phone cards, which annoyed some people. There was always niggling pressure as the union had its own second-hand bookshop also selling sugary sweets and lollies of all descriptions. There had always been and still is a Wednesday market day set up by outsiders who paid a nominal rent to the union, even though they were outside the union's pseudo bounds. An American-style fresh fruit outlet was set up near the chemistry building and was there for years.

All of this brought more people to the area, and thus improved our chances of success. Our sales probably rose some twenty per cent and photographics also boomed, helped by having a small counter near the front which took in countless bags of developing and processing. Behind it in Kodak yellow we had shelving for a selection of Kodak film and the occasional Agfa and Fuji products. We stocked a couple of instamatic cameras. This was when Polaroid was being phased out with digital imaging yet to come.

Alex built the counters to increase the stock displayed providing us with an overall increase in point-of-sale opportunities. We had the largest sales of Boots' Strepsils lozenges for a private pharmacy in Australia and almost the country's largest photo processing outlet. Kodak was making overtures suggesting we process our own photos in the pharmacy.

We kept in touch with the St Lucia Pharmacy owner over the occasional problem with customer accounts, which was very useful for both of us. He was a funny man who had studied pharmacy after accountancy. Suddenly, he decided to close the pharmacy because of declining sales and to retire, and that was that. For us it translated as a twenty per cent increase in business on top of what we already had in our new locale.

We sold two houses in Toowoomba and a unit on Coronation Drive. As the Brisbane one had been an off-the-plan purchase, it made a very good profit thanks to Gillian, who had spotted it under construction while a patient at the Wesley Hospital.

SPORTING EDUCATION

Sara and Peter never attended public-funded education. Both started their formative years in grade one at St Peter's Lutheran College. It is a typically modern German Lutheran school in a prime location at Indooroopilly.

Peter left in year five and went to Brisbane Boys' College at Toowong. Sara stayed on and struggled more with the learning modules. She left in year eight to go to Somerville House in South Brisbane, a sister school to BBC. Mrs Koch was St Peter's junior school headmistress, and that is enough said except parents were urged to get the pronunciation correct. St Peter's is a GPS school for sport for girls only and in those days a TSS school for boys, which is a lower rung on the competitive ladder. We had thought of sending Sara to Ironside State School, but with my sister Narelle there as a good year seven teacher we thought that was an unwise choice.

Mr Einersen, a sports master at St Peter's, said that he had never seen anyone with Peter's natural ability for tennis. But tennis was low on the agenda at St Peter's so eventually they appointed me as a tennis coach to improve their girls' and boys' tennis hopes.

One afternoon I met a reverend military major who was

watching his daughter and I saw he was using a computer. He mentioned it had the unusual name of Apple. Computers were now coming into wide use and St Peter's was at the academic forefront in that respect.

With tennis, you can only coach someone so much, and without natural ability and the right psychological approach, there is no progression. But it is still a good recreational sport. I helped the school for the love of tennis, as I did not rely upon the income. While coaching at St Peter's I rummaged around and found some old tennis shields and they gave me permission to have my father French polish them. They were never used. Basketball, swimming and netball became the go-to sports on that campus, but mostly swimming. To this day it remains as a very successful Olympic coaching facility for swimming. Gold and silver medallists have many times trained in its pools.

It was around this time that I was coaching a few families with children keen to learn. I made many friends. At one place, the owner had a glass wall as a practice board to hit against. A flying stone from the gardener's motor mower gave it a few noticeable cracks over time. The eldest daughter sadly died from breast cancer only a few years later.

When Sara went to Somerville House, the deputy headmaster from St Peter's moved there at the same time to become headmaster. Carson Dron remained as headmaster at St Peter's but was someone I did not engage much with. Sara made several friends there including one named Alison, whose parents we knew via a Bill Lyster who loved his tennis. He lived at Chapel Hill and entertained a lot with a barbecue beside the pool, as people did in those days. He lived not far from Mac Lethbridge (Lethbridge and Munro), the solicitor who had done much of the conveyancing for our many houses.

During one late afternoon barbecue at Bill Lyster's house his daughter lost her contact lens while swimming. I looked in the pool and to my surprise could see it at the bottom. Her brother still remembers the occasion even today.

MORE ON EDUCATION

Bill Lyster was a likeable character and was full of ideas on how to make it rich. He died before his staircase lift idea came to fruition. Around the late 1980s he encouraged me to join Tattersalls Tennis, then the actual Tattersalls Club, a few years later.

Matters of his estate were handled by a friend and confidante named Ian Revie, who then became our accountant before we parted ways further down the track. Ian played at Tattersalls and had an office at Toowong, where he sat at a desk for years before branching out on his own, buying an old house at Toowong and trading as an accountant from there. He had a tennis court at Bourbong Street in Chapel Hill. I might have played there only once. At his previous office was another accountant, Mike Handy, also one dabbling in retailing rather than sticking to his profession. His brother Chris Handy played rugby for Australia and later was a commentator for many years. Mike often popped in unannounced at our Chapel Hill house, imagining he had been followed by police and to avoid being breathalysed. He had many times visited us at Twinkle House at Marcoola and spent lavishly on seafood, including oysters and pipis. His lighting business turned off and his marriage broke up and for at least two years he vindictively claimed I had not paid fees for faked timed hours. He used debt collectors' notices and harassing phone calls from Bundaberg Collectors, who were no doubt acquaintances. It was during all this stress that by chance I mentioned all this when talking to Mac Lethbridge, and he said 'Ignore it, he's doing the same to others.'

Toowong Village shopping centre once had a car park at the top with nothing to prevent anyone going over the edge and hitting the concrete several floors below. It was on that concrete that that his body was apparently found. His former wife, Roz, is still around and for a time rented or owned a house next to our demolished one in Harts Road. It was there that we met Roz's sister, who is the wife of Screw Turner, the owner of Flight Centre. Screw was a vet who started TipTop Travel in the late sixties and early seventies. He has never looked back.

This was not far from many houses with tennis courts, including Boopie and Lynda Porter, Sandy Mayne and the beautiful house with the glass wall hitting board, all adjacent to the St Peter's precinct. Sandy passed quickly away as a result of aggressive melanoma skin cancer, only a few years ago. We used to see her walking around the university when we were doing the same.

* * *

PRIVATE SCHOOLS ARE HOT beds for wealthy people, working people and religious people to a lesser extent. Life is the best educator of all and family is paramount. There is nowhere more competitive than on the field of a private secondary school. It is steeped in the public-school history of the United Kingdom, from which it took its lead many years ago.

The oldest GPS is Ipswich Grammar School (IGS), which is totally surprising given the present day demographics of suburbs close to Ipswich. The Roman Catholic school system takes a bit of beating with placing their strict denominational schools strategically in different socio-economic demographics. Gregory Terrace and Nudgee College are GPSs who are members and numerous others are secondary tier, though Downlands at Toowoomba really should be a GPS. Rumour has it that the two other Catholic GPSs are opposed to that. Even with competition among parents, competition with schools internally and externally, somehow students excel in sport and academia. But to watch the helicopter parents is a delightful thing as they lobby teachers for their sons or daughters to get into a school's higher representative team. It is really at an art-form level. They should wear a pocket on their blazer. And now infiltrating in increasing numbers are those from India and Sri Lanka, China and Asia in general. This is the ego at work.

INVESTING AND ACCOUNTANTS

Probably the most significant thing that I did when living at Harts Road, Indooroopilly, was to start buying shares.

There is an old saying that if you invest in shares and negatively geared property, if you need to sell up it is easier by a country mile to sell shares. You can sell a proportion or the lot. Whereas with a house, you really can't sell off the front steps to get some much-needed cash. Whilst some might say this is bleedingly obvious, few investors see it that way as many do not understand shares and opt for a tax-incentivised loan to buy a house.

Buying government bonds is another form of investment of a sort, but the only time I did that was when it was required to set up a self-managed super fund. This was at a time, and I stand to be corrected, that Paul Keating was encouraging the creation of self-managed super funds for retirement and giving tax-based incentives to do so. Thus the establishment of your own super fund required setting up a limited company compliant with ATO requirements. Accountants began diversifying from their normal bean counting role, to the super area. For the average worker, and I mean no disrespect, it was not an option, and still is not.

The theory was that the super fund would be your self-funded pension fund upon retirement. This was saving government pensions for only those who were means tested and therefore supposedly more in need of retirement assistance. I think most people would agree this has ballooned into quite a complex area.

We had experienced home loan interest rates of sixteen per cent and higher. Had I known about it then this would have made me aware that investing in shares was a better option. Another well-known adage is that money makes money. This is the absolute obvious truth.

Remember, way back there had been Poseidon shares with many people losing money when the price crashed. I was aware of that when I bought my first shares when CSL was privatised. I felt my knowledge of the CSL production line of things such as flu injections and plasma products made this a safe bet. The IPO cost was around $2.40 a share. This has been a stellar share under the stewardship of McNamee and others and today it is a global entity.

It was a time in Australia when much thought was given to privatising companies. Telstra was one such and the Commonwealth Bank of Australia another. Everyone put their hand up by registering their intention of purchasing the new share offerings. Telstra did it in tranches, and you had to make a value judgement as to when to buy and how many.

Shares are a gamble and the mum and dad investors hopped on the bandwagon and it became a free for all. People who owned shares had never done so before nor knew what to do when they actually received a certificate confirming ownership. This was the time when you even received a deed of ownership for each cash outlay. I have to thank my son Peter who one day advised me to keep a good record of each purchase and how much was paid. He created an Excel spreadsheet for me.

He already had his Bachelor of Business and was at a firm called Manning Hixson and Melitz, working with a good group of people including a tax expert. Peter was doing his chartered accounting years at the time and had a regular girlfriend from Toowoomba. There was another whose parents had an avocado farm, around the Ipswich way. He would retreat there to study for exams and was successful in passing all at the specified times.

Peter clearly had an urge to travel and one day Gillian and I met him for lunch at a Japanese restaurant in Anzac Square in the city. He asked if we would mind if he applied for a banking job overseas. He felt he could not remain at his best in an office environment. Parents should never stand in the way of their children and we agreed it was a good idea. With Gillian's parents and family in the UK, he could touch base with them if need be. He became a regular visitor to Monica and linked up with second cousin Simon Gunson, with whom he remains friends today.

It was around this time that a company offered their services as an accountant for our business. We became close friends with various members of the firm for a few years, even going to Hong Kong with the firm for a conference on investing. We all splurged on tailored suits which the Indian street traders were happy to provide, offering extra trousers and the usual cheaper yet better fabrics and so on. I still have some of those moth-eaten suits and the coat hangers on which they came. By this time Gillian knew her way around Hong Kong as we had been there so many times. We had taken Peter and Sara there to experience a different culture.

Peter headed out of the quite cheap Park Hotel as quickly as possible and I recall showing him the live prawns and small crabs for sale in the open air. Nathan Road was always where we went for Gillian to go shopping, especially in shoe shops and a very good leather shop situated down one end. Opposite was a McDonald's, which was just so busy with schoolchildren wearing their omnipresent dark blue uniforms scoffing a hamburger and chips and a milkshake after school. Close by was a Baptist church and everything was hustle and bustle. Hong Kong was still a British colony. I recall huge fish being filleted and fried in front of you. It was the first time we experienced large tanks (with often some dead fish in them) from which you could choose your meal – lobsters, crayfish, mussels, large and small crabs, it was all there. But they did not have chilli crab, which was something we were to experience with Peter and Stephanie a few years later when they were working in a much cleaner Singapore where a death sentence was the penalty for drug importation, whipping was for misdemeanours and chewing gum was a definite no. Raffles Hotel was the place to go and traditionally throw your empty peanut shells on the floor.

We found out about the New Territories fish markets from Ronnie Woodhouse. He had a friend living in Hong Kong who took us there by train after his work. We took Gillian's sister, Angela, once, and a few times we met up with her and

Monica at the Park Hotel. It was there that we had a great time. Salmon was in excessive supply so I stacked our little bar fridge with spares and Gillian brought some bread rolls from the dinner table – and that was lunch done for the next day. Sometimes this was supplemented with assorted cheeses, which was how to travel cheaply. At one meeting with Angela in Hong Kong she walked ahead of me with Gillian and said she had discovered her eldest daughter was gay. It was no surprise to us as we had never thought otherwise.

It was a time when the Hong Kong rugby sevens tournament had a huge following, which is no longer the case. I seemed to be like some sort of a father figure to many of Peter's friends, and we went to Penfold's rugby lunches at Ballymore to raise funds for the Reds Rugby. Accountants used their spare funds to go to and organize sporting events, and so we once visited a Polo match, with champagne and trimmings, where we sat and were totally bored. We did not know many people in their firm's marquee, but it was nice to be asked.

As our journey progressed, we acquired shares in AMP at a time when we were able to convert to shares what we had owned in life insurances. We, rather I, still had the shares until recently when we decided to convert them to a much better share, Eagers Automotive.

One firm encouraged us in share purchases and suggested we borrow money to purchase shares at a later time. The money borrowed was held against the share security and, whilst it got you started, it was like negatively gearing for a house. The difference was that the asset was the shares that hopefully you had bought with due diligence. This firm was also instrumental (and it was the right thing to do) in setting up a superannuation fund for retirement and this also had great tax benefits. Family trusts were in vogue at the time and we had one for a few years before we cancelled it when living at Kawana Waters. All the shares or most of them could be traded across from the named owner to the super fund as long as they were at the market value at the time.

There came a time when, with the borrowed cash, we were able to buy blue chip shares and encouraged us go into managed funds such as Platinum Asia and others. The catch with funds management was that when you sat down and worked it out, the fees being charged were exorbitant and the financial year statement was often in negative territory. A whole host of people were employed all dipping in for expenses against the capital you invested. On top of that, we were being hit with more consultancy fees for returns. The day of dawning came when an annual fee arrived just for a casual conversation over a lunchtime at Tattersalls Club.

Eventually I refused to pay and things got really messy, to a point of a Mexican stand-off with outright threats to go to court. In the end I turned to Ian, an accountant (deceased) who had a small business and who should, and did, charge less for superannuation returns. He eventually confronted the exorbitant fees charged on our behalf after costing out his work, about the money he claimed was owed to them in fees by the super fund. He actually visited the suits, as he called them, and went through his costings compared with the regulated costings. He did a great job for us which was and is still appreciated.

It would appear that things could turn nasty, so it was best to agree to a settlement of the reduced fees. My advise to anyone getting friendly with money managers, financial planners, bank managers mortgage, brokers and accountants is to always be wary of their charge out rates. Even a casual beer, which you may have paid for, could be linked to a hefty time charge

Revie was laid back and somewhat casual in his approach but did our returns for a few years and covered an ATO audit, which no doubt had been orchestrated, though no one ever knows who by. I played tennis with Ian and also with Billie Lyster. In the end I found that Ian had staff who I felt were not supporting him where his clients were concerned. They apparently lost my car's mileage logbook at a time when I was not disposed towards forgiveness and I told them to get off their bums and find it. When the head of a small firm or any organisation is called out, the people behind them always, and naturally, close ranks and so they nicely tell you to piss off. A GP practice can be the same.

There were other firms, and our last accountants were Johnston Rorke, who had a niche market as specialists in pharmacy. Bruce Annabel was a nice ulta-marathon runner, along with his physiotherapist partner who had developed a niche Pharmacy Accountancy practice set-up, which he then passed on to another.

I decided to use my own managerial judgement from years of experience, which was far in excess of firms going after niche businesses. They were not pharmacists, so they came up with things like succession plans and no end of shop designs. They were your marketers, and at the same time any cost-benefit analysis was not worth the fee to secure it. They also were in the business of selling pharmacies, doing deals with banks and wholesalers. Yes, you should do group buys with your pharmacy friends who are competing against you. There was no end to their imagination for fee generation.

We met with a retired old school accountant just after we had sold Campus Pharmacy, and he had some succession planning advice which he did not charge for! Always buy banks, keep some cash, and you'll have enough to retire on. He had also bought a Porsche 911. The other fellow did as he was aiming for his own niche partnership at the time. A born-again new-age accountant. For some fifteen years or so we have used Brittons Chartered Accountants. They are small but obliging and do the job for us very cost effectively and they no doubt will retire as we all do!

There was a young guy from Peter's BBC school days by the name of Michael (Mickey) Baker. A nice guy, small of stature, he once walked all the way from the city and we found him the next day sleeping in our driveway at Toowong. They are still good friends. Michael suggested to Pete that he knew of a good firm in the city, ABN AMRO Morgans, that managed super funds and had a partner named Hamish Dee.

Some accountants, as I am, are somewhat sceptical of financial planners, and on that I certainly agreed. Mortgage brokers were totally worse in many ways. Nevertheless, we made contact with Hamish and over time we established a reasonable relationship. We still use Hamish at Morgans which has grown to be probably the largest company of its type in Australia. This is a stockbroking company trading in shares and investment strategies. Currently we have an extremely good relationship, and we manage all our own investments. That way, you can only blame yourself if something goes wrong.

Hamish just offers advice on IPOs and chatting is always a good thing when share investing. Mickie Baker had worked with them and so putting everything together we matched it all up for them to be our brokers. It is a company with several members having gone to protestant schools, and has a linked arrangement with DDH Graham, who is linked with BOQ, in a sub-bank arrangement, thus offering better cash investment rates for clients of Morgans.

David Graham loved his tennis and started this up many years ago. He is an old boy of CEGS.

Investing and accounting are a symbiotic relationship and feed off small and large businesses. The very large businesses are still in Sydney and Melbourne, and Brisbane still has its own CBD, but it is not quite up with the others where the old boys' clubs rule the roost. This has changed as the old girls' clubs are taking their place. No one should be denied a directorship because of gender, race, colour or creed, but should be appointed solely on merit.

Australia is a small player that punches above its weight. But for minerals and enormous quantities of uranium we have nothing, except a population of twenty-six million, which is fewer than Texas. The real players in investments are in London, New York and Singapore with Beijing lurking with good GDP now reduced post-Covid. Yet China is regarded as a third world country by the UN.

FAMILY MATTERS

It is now January 2024 and as hot and sticky as it often can be in Brisbane as we suffer with a heatwave and humidity.

So what makes a family? Well, it is when you ask occasionally for some assistance to sort out a problem. This was the case just yesterday with the air conditioning. Our son came around and helped solve the problem. This is the weekend and no one in the trades works on a weekend. Naturally essential services do, but Parliament always has an extended break from December to February. This does not happen in Asian countries where they keep powering on.

We are a nation governed mostly by trade unions who currently have locked down our export industries to a large extent. They did this in both world wars.

Not even the military can be stirred too much to help in catastrophes such as the cyclone just after we visited Cairns in October. That is why I say we punch above our weight and place much emphasis on Australia's prowess in various sports. We are a sporting nation, which is not such a bad thing.

Our children, Sara and Peter, have married with Sara the first to dive into that abyss. The marriage is now in a state of flux, with the eldest grandchild, Jackson, soon to turn eighteen and hopefully make a success of his chosen future in horticulture. Her second child, Oscar, has two years to go at a private school before plunging into his chosen career. He seems much attuned to the area of business, so let him put his best foot forward. Oscar recently returned to school for the first term of 2024.

We have supported Sara with her unaffordable costs, which has recently increased with the economy the way it currently is. Brisbane is a small world and I knew her previous landlord as I signed off on his practical dispensary work in his final year at Campus Pharmacy. What a negatively geared small world, if you'll excuse the sarcasm.

Peter is for all intents and purposes happily married to Stephanie Rascoe. They have two delightful children, one boy and one girl. Cooper is quite an athlete as is Zoe who has oozed personality from the day she was born. Cooper was in the junior development squad with Chelsea in the UK when they lived there. Zoe was born in Canada. Both children have a multitude of passports as their parents travelled for some twenty-five years with business appointments. Cooper is at BBC and has started term 1 for 2024. Zoe is at Somerville House.

Sara was a good runner and competed in tennis and cross country while at Somerville. She completed a BSc, majoring in psychology after first trying nursing for a year. She was for a time a House Boarding Mistress at St Ursula's in Toowoomba after boarding at a place known as Dodgy House, near the University of Southern Queensland. Peter also went to USQ and graduated with a business degree majoring in accounting and later became chartered. He gained a half blue for tennis while at USQ.

Peter was told by many people that he was a gifted tennis player, but especially by Mr Einersen at St Peter's and later by Reverend Bradley, who took junior tennis at BBC. It was clear that the tennis exposure there was too uncompetitive and allowed his enthusiasm to be lost, so we encouraged him to play in state age titles. He excelled at that and was eventually chosen to join the McDonald's elite tennis players squad. This was based at Carseldine, where Ashley Cooper's tennis centre still remains. A few times I coached there when they sent the word out that they were short of my level of experience.

The good thing about tennis is that you can usually play it for most of your life. I tried to introduce wheelchair tennis at Milton TC but it fell on deaf ears. Now wheelchair tennis has national titles around the world with its own grand slam events.

When Sara left St Peter's for Somerville the Rev Bradley provided a reference for her to gain enrolment at her new school. She played a little tennis in the age tournaments but was more interested in riding horses and the aforementioned pony which she named Twinkle Toes. I walked her down to Fig Tree Pocket Pony Club many Saturdays as the feisty pony might shy at any moment at a passing car. She was good at riding, with helmet, her own saddle and riding strides and introduced son Jackson likewise hoping he would gain self-confidence similar to her own. Life experiences and exposure to different things are held in your children's memories and hopefully will be passed on. That is the theory and in our case it worked pretty well, except no one has followed tennis in pursuit of excellence in that sport. But dispositions change as people marry and skills and intelligence follow their own genetic paths. None are bank tellers, if you can excuse my reiteration of that long ago time at the Taringa State School.

Studying is now momentously different from our own days, as there is much more pressure to achieve if parents allow this to occur. Referencing is easier as information abounds on the internet whereas in our day it meant going to the print edition of the *Encyclopaedia Britannica* and looking in the alphabetical volumes. My parents could never afford them so I learnt the best way as others of my era did, from teachers and life experiences. I recall neck hair rising from the sound of scratchy chalk on a blackboard, and a duster often in pink or white, depending on the chalk being used to be erased. They made great missiles for teachers to use when attention lagged. Rooms were not air conditioned, and when I went to university and sat in a staggered well-made lecture theatre, the cool was something to really remember. Noticeably, no one cared if you decided to walk out of a lecture. The years have rolled by for the children and hopefully soon they will be independent so that we can enjoy our retirement, in a cost-effective way.

I have learned never to listen to other people's success stories and their supposed wealth. I have met hundreds who talk the talk and invariably they are walking the walk with inherited money, or by sheer luck. We are unlikely to encounter those on a government pension during our holiday journeys. Our best friends fill this category and there is no separation by wealth by either side. I could not give a damn what someone has as long as we are quite comfortable, and becoming quite comfortable is not by wasting money but by taking risks, which is where the risk capital terminology evolved.

Even the most intelligent people fall by the wayside during life's journey, whether they choose to or not. Like sport, you have to have the stamina to guts it out and turn the other cheek when slapped in the face, with the sting still lingering and tingling. I believe this is based on a quote from the Bible which my mother used when I was a child.

* * *

IN 2005 TUYET PHAM had been working for us as a pharmacist for a couple of years. She was a good pharmacist, not like the strange person before her whose parents were serving five years in jail for fraud. I was just about to sack him for his laziness when I heard from the CBA that he was looking to buy a pharmacy in Tasmania.

I will never forget the fax machine suddenly coming alive with the paper offering his written resignation. I had been hoping that with some convoluted advice that he was my ideal person for succession planning. But he was often late for work on his Lambretta, having had an accident or two. Then he was admitted to hospital with meningitis (so I was told) and his pharmacist wife could not step in as she had children to look after. The children were encouraged by him to play in mud puddles, which he created. They were completely naked under their house, as happy as a busy bee or nest building wasp in the mud. Their rented house was untidy to boot, which should have rung alarm bells right at the outset. I was also warned by his previous employer, and the Boots representative, that he was well known as being unreliable, and frankly somewhat lazy.

For a while I had had a new pharmacist from north Queensland who arrived wearing a safari suit for her interview. Her female partner was studying at UQ, hence the incentive for her to apply for the position. That ended when her American partner broke up with her, which was very upsetting for her. Of similar ilk, and a lovely person, the CBA senior manager at that time gave her advice on where to meet others, including perhaps basketball, where she met someone from the police academy, as I recall. The same CBA manager sat down and held my hand to comfort me when she thought one of my parents had died.

After all this came Tuyet, a successful refugee from South Vietnam whose sister had been shot and wounded by the Viet Cong. Mike, her husband, was a steadying influence towards our culture and so it was that after many hints from us she suddenly turned around and made us an offer for the pharmacy we could not refuse. **Game, set and match.** We remain friends to this day and we often see her at the pharmacy near Graceville. Her children, born when she was our employee, are quite successful, one at university and one studying medicine.

I mentioned Mike was a steadying cultural influence, and boy did we need it to pursue the sale. Their solicitor was acting for them and stocktakes had to be done when Tuyet was still manager of Campus Pharmacy. It is a complex process to sell a business on a university campus, especially when someone stocked up excessively, which in turn reduced the net value of the agreed purchase price. I well remember how Tuyet lost it on settlement day when she had come to remove any expired drugs, or those that had only a thirty-day expiry. Those with a thirty-day expiry were perfectly capable of being dispensed as they were popular brands. Our biggest seller and dispensed item was the oral contraceptive, which was then Diane 35 ED. Any arrangement we had with the then supplier via the Schering representative was what we had negotiated, and therefore it was argued that it was up to the purchaser to negotiate their own arrangement.

They may have wished to change to a generic brand in certain products, which were more profitable insofar as purchase price was concerned. Solicitors handling a pharmacy sale need to be well and truly conversant with more specialised detail than the average conveyancer is used to. Any bonus stock not paid for but gained by smart buying is rightfully the owner's stock. We also had Musashi products which were meticulously checked for use-by dates, as were energy drinks. Gillian stuck to her guns and in the end we were left with a pile outside the shop of so-called disputed goods. Considering the petty value of the products we said, 'Okay, delete them from the official stocktake figures'.

The $250 000 Kodak digital printer was included for obvious reasons at a reduced price in the depreciation schedule of stock, goods and chattels compiled by the agreed neutral stocktake company, who provided Pharmacy Guild representatives with appropriate accreditation if a dispute went to court.

What was really going on as a preliminary to the final nod of approval from both parties was a natural and huge degree of anxiety about the final transfer of money after the initial deposit was paid for the thirty-day contract. We would never have signed anything that might require determining or supportive third-party wholesaler funding as that can be an easy way out. The contract of sale was financially unconditional from the outset. The rest was the hard part, with a Vietnamese woman who would barter to the absolute limit, even welling into tears at one stage. This was when we had a chat with her husband Mike who, although he knew nothing about pharmacies, knew about money.

Determining the value was hard enough for a unique pharmacy, which on a wet day sold as many as three or four hundred umbrellas. Rainbird was the most popular brand, with collapsible ones also favoured, and the occasional large one. The Asians would ask for rain shields and we would oblige if we had any in stock. We were also the darlings of the company Johnson and Johnson, as we were a huge account for tampons, Meds being the largest seller. The day-after pill was also a big seller and there were restrictions for counselling associated with the labelling. The other large seller was Ventolin (Salbutamol), which was in huge demand during westerly days when dust was blown and pollen filled the air. Customers were advised it was only a temporary relief.

In the end, the short expiry date items were taken back and a substantial amount of what she did not wish to have we took to our home at Twickenham Street where we stored it in the downstairs study.

The day we took the stock over to Nelson's pharmacy at Stafford was somewhat surreal and he welcomed the miscellaneous items from us. On the way home on a long hill in Red Hill I was stopped for being over the speed limit even though I had the Mercedes C Class on cruise control. That pissed me off as I drove off past the Catholic schools that dotted the area, where Irish settlers had originally settled after the potato famine in Ireland.

Remember the expensive Kodak machine? Well we popped in one day not long after the sale, as I still used to give Tuyet some business, and saw it in a dumpster outside as their sales no longer warranted its use. They had decided to change the fit-out and use its space for other items such as vitamins.

* * *

THE SENSE OF RELIEF was palpable in 2005 as we finally finished with retail pharmacy. I had had enough of it and could see where it was going with the discount chains and the like. It is now quite a wonder how they can coexist, especially as none are in supermarkets, as is the case in other parts of the world.

The pharmacy had been our retirement superannuation nest egg and from here it was still onward and upward without having to be bullied by Commonwealth and state governments in the crazy duplicity of the system.

In 2017, at Heathrow Airport, I pushed a bag with my leg at the carousel and suddenly everything went ape shit. I had torn my meniscus and struggled on home to Brisbane via Virgin Atlantic, using a wheelchair complete with flag to board the aircraft. I was loaded into another chair during the break at

Hong Kong. It was a struggle for the woman pushing me and I saw parts of the terminal I never knew existed.

The first thing I did was to go to the Wesley emergency service where the orthopaedic registrar eventually saw what I was talking about through his tired drooping eyes. He gave me a referral to an orthopaedic surgeon, named Scott Somerville, who was an unhappy man as a student at BBC.

I woke up in theatre with him in a negative pressure space suit and cracking jokes with the Canadian anaesthetist while sawing my left leg into two. This was an experience to behold before more anaesthetic went into my spinal block and I awakened later in the ward. It was like the way a plumber would wrestle with a pipe and insert glue after joining two pieces of PVC together. With a total knee replacement, sterility before and afterwards was paramount, and I was anxious about that.

We were now living in Graceville and the long road to recovery meant learning to walk again but I had some good physiotherapists near the hospital. No one knows what you go through during rehabilitation. I remember later looking through the wire at the Tennyson Tennis Centre at the players hitting up during the Queensland titles and thinking all I was ever going to be able to do would be to look. However, with a few years under my belt and a return to Allsports Physiotherapy at Indooroopilly, I was able to get going and play again. But it was purely social and very dissatisfying. The anger that wells into one's psyche is immense to say the least.

I played with beginners at Morningside and tried to form my own group at UQ on Wednesday afternoons. The vast majority of them were arseholes, but I joined with Walter, the German at Mount Ommaney for a few years and relatively recently retired from there. That was hard, but not a bad idea. The heat was taking its toll and the number of good players was dwindling. On a few occasions I was hit in the back of the head with a ball which sent me spinning. I remember lying on a seat at Indooroopilly High School where the last such incident happened and looking up at the cursed crows and saying, 'It's not time you mother f*99ers'. The ambulance came and it was off to the Wesley again to be diagnosed with vertigo induced blood pressure. The ambos inserted a drip as my blood pressure was very low while the ECG seemed okay so far as they were concerned.

But was there something else going on which had caused this? So I later did a stress test at the Wesley with a Dr Rainbird. He stopped it at 150 bpm and told me I could lose some weight.

I was still playing nigh on three years ago when Peter and family returned to Australia with the onslaught of the pandemic to be quarantined and live here permanently.

When they left their quarantine hotel in the city, all four moved to a house with beautiful roses where Stephanie said I must be mad to play in the heat. Intermittently, in the earlier years, we travelled to places such as Norfolk Island, Bali (we went once before the Bali Bombings and as time flies, returning recently) and Tasmania, and continued taking holidays on the Sunshine Coast. All this was done while managing our superannuation fund because we had reached the retirement phase of the pension.

RETIREMENT YEARS

When Gillian's parents were alive we travelled to the UK and also visited Peter and family in the various places they were based. We did not know if they were coming back to Australia as they were well settled in places including Singapore, Toronto and the UK.

We were present in Toronto when Zoe was born, and what a great moment that was to see our first and only granddaughter. Cooper was born in Sydney and while I was in hospital with my knee replacement Gillian flew down there to see them. Peter came to see me in hospital shortly after Cooper was born. He is now in grade eight at BBC.

As for Sara's two boys, one is turning eighteen years (Jackson) and Oscar is in year eleven at ATCL. Since Sara's marriage ended in a messy way, those remnants of support continue as I write in January 2024.

We visited many places in our retirement years, starting with Western Australia in 2006. Paris was one of my favourites, as was Hong Kong, staying at the Langham Hotel. We have flown countless times around the world, with our favourite airline being Virgin Atlantic out of Sydney, which is a pain in the arse when transferring between domestic and international travel terminals. Hearing an airport boarding call to some overseas destination still arouses the thrill of travelling and sends a shiver down my spine!

* * *

From the very early travels, if a game of tennis was likely, the racquets were brought along.

The Epsom District Hospital Tennis Association in Carshalton, Surrey, was my first overseas club experience. I was invited to join with a few others including a county player, and we won the premiership for which I have a tiny trophy somewhere.

The Canadian Toronto Tennis Club where Peter was a champion member was really nice and friendly. I played doubles once, but those guys were just too good. They were excellent sportsman.

In Germany's Black Forest region I played at a private club on clay as part of a team from Tatts and we lost to the local club which had a lovely clay court and turned on a barbecue with desserts such as Black Forest cake and so many other delights that it was embarrassing to eat so much. We toured the area and found Freiburg (founded circa 1120) with its cobbled streets was a delight. All but its cathedral tower was flattened during the Second World War. We caught trains from Stuttgart to Cologne and on to Brugge. Gillian had her birthday in Stuttgart, and we also sold the Twickenham Street house by phone to Mary from Ray White Graceville. We had been renting it for $890 a week and the renters decided they wanted to buy it. Gillian thought long and hard and did the math, and between us we said, 'Sell'. It was too good a price to ignore even while being on the phone in the city where Mercedes headquarters is located.

From when I first worked at QMH to more recent times, I have visited the All England Tennis Club in Wimbledon to watch and enjoy. I have never been to Roland Garros in Paris or New York's Arthur Ashe stadium. Peter has been to them all.

I have played a few times at the Toowoomba Tennis Centre during interclub tennis, and the Toowoomba players are always good, and difficult to defeat. Peter assisted at the Tennyson Tennis Centre to beat them by reverse year two. The reception and presentation afterwards were at the Brisbane Club, which was lovely.

The Boar's Head tennis club in Charlottesville, USA, shows why American tennis is so strong. I had a few games there with Peter a few years back. We stayed for a few days as Steph had friends and relatives close by. This was notably the last time I ventured into a bath, because of my shoulders.

I coached at the Milton Tennis Centre, Frew Park, Milton, and Cooper's Tennis Centre, Carseldine, for a while and played a few times at the Tennyson Tennis Centre, including when centre court was converted to clay. Tennis was social here as it was at Morningside Tennis Centre.

At first I was sorry to give up tennis, but this has been more than compensated for by following the grandchildren's sporting exploits.

TRAVEL DIARY

Since 2006 we have travelled far and wide, much of which is covered in the Hunt-Sharp family blog. The detail is meticulous, for that is the sort of person I am when it comes to recording our travel exploits. It is not about boasting, as the blog is closed to the public.

BLOG ARCHIVE (SHOWING THEIR RELATIVE NUMBERS):

- 2024 (1) – CURRENT Seaborne coastline of Australia, South Australia
- 2023 (25) Medical Episode
- 2022 (74) Making the most of lockdown
- 2021 (122) Versace Gold Coast; Covid pandemic
- 2020 (23) Family and the Covid pandemic
- 2019 (33) Middle East, India, Jordan and Israel by ship, our nicest trip
- 2018 (223) Singapore and Darwin via Indonesia with seaborne foodie moments
- 2017 (91) Family important occasions
- 2016 (72) Somerset, UK, and France
- 2015 (108) Family and New Zealand (lava glass)

- 2014 (154) Family; Pete and I played and won easily at Morningside Tennis Centre.
- 2013 (178) Family photos at home
- 2012 (195) St Mary's Anglican Church, Brisbane, with christening of Zoe day after they arrived back
- 2011 (168) Toronto where Peter and Stephanie lived. Fairytale photos
- 2010 (106) France, Calvados region and Rouen (first time)
- 2009 (236) Clem 7 Brisbane tunnel walk before the opening
- 2008 (64) New Zealand
- 2007 (234) Seven months in Europe and UK. Paris August 2007
- 2006 (100) Western Australia

FOOD AND DRINK

Indians in the lower caste parts of India consume meals on pressed metal trays, made in their millions for that specific purpose. They might chuck a bit of meat to man's best friend, their dog, while picking their teeth and muttering in some Indian dialect. Otherwise, it is a case of tucking into the steamy hot meal and forgetting the flies or scorpions nearby. The metal trays have one indent for rice, one for chutney and one for naan bread, with pappadums dropped on top. A larger metal indentation is there for some form of meat or chicken curry. Carbohydrates come mostly from the naan. The whole dish is easy to wash after giving scraps to the local dog, while avoiding any sacred cows.

I have watched people in the Indian quarters of cities in various parts of the world and marvelled at the way they can sit cross-legged, with their tin plate of food in front of them on a cushion. They methodically devour everything by hand. They seem not to feel the heat or humidity.

Their freshly squeezed pineapple juice is rather nice, especially when they make it for you as you stand in front of their roadside stall. Ice is an option, which will come as the depositing of a couple of cubes by hand, which you accept with gratitude, because it is so hot. Do they wash their hands? Well it is best not to think too much about that. Most tourists' impression of India is that they have to accept diarrhoea and/or vomiting as rites of passage. It is more the type of food that causes diarrhoea rather than lack of cleanliness, depending on where you eat. Five star hotels should be okay as long as the kitchens are clean and policed by local authorities. This is why Singapore is a good destination as the authorities ensure very clean establishments with food outlets regularly inspected and allotted a rating. A score of eighty-five per cent or higher results in an A, and the lowest grade is a D, which ranges from forty to forty-nine per cent, which is a pass. These grades are required to be displayed on hawker stands.

In recent years our Food and Health Department in Brisbane had a similar, so called original, system using a star rating. After a while, no one took any notice.

Hawker food centres in Penang, Hong Kong and particularly Singapore are cooked food centres which are amazing places to visit, usually in the evening, with jugs of Singha beer to wash things down. Upgrading or reconstruction of hawker centres was initiated in Singapore in the 1990s.

The bread in Singapore is superb and ours is a monopolised disgrace. The French bread is the finest, as are that country's cheeses. Nothing is better than having bread sliced in front of you by hand as the boulangerie does with much aplomb. And the almond croissants are magnifique. Patisseries are generally separate to the bakery.

Brugge, in Belgium, is historically closely aligned to Burgundy in France and has exceptional cakes and bread, with mostly only real cream used in the most perfect of sponge cakes. A slice of apple tart and real whipped cream with a lovely coffee is the morning experience before searching where to go for an evening meal of mussels in white wine slightly warmed because of the cool evenings. Burgundy pies are a real delight and there could be as many as twenty beers to choose from with pure blonde Duvel or Kwak very popular choices. Brown beer, Cuvee du Chateau Kasteel, is excellent for making Guinness pie.

Then there's the Irish pub. The Irish have internationally acclaimed cooking schools, which produce some of the finest pastry chefs. It is worth noting their yummy patisseries and macarons are cheaper than in France.

Cheeses in Australia are mostly good, but astronomically expensive for local brands, where cow's milk is used by retailers as a price point sale item at the expense of the dairy farmers.

In India, generally houses are spotless inside. In the rural areas you see demonstrated one way they achieve cleanliness. Everything that is not needed is thrown out on the side of an often-dusty road, to be collected. There are no bins, so crows and rats have a whale of a time. It's very quirky and dirty by Western standards as young boys played cricket on the dusty street and stepped aside as our vehicle passed them. They are a great cricketing nation, where gambling is not frowned upon.

Singapore, which has a large Indian population, also has its own Indian brothel quarter. This is the oldest profession, and it knows no boundaries in race or creed. Visit Pompeii in Italy if possible to see the brothel quarter, which is absolutely stunning from a societal perspective.

G&T AND OTHER DELIGHTS

I had my first gin and tonic on a small cabin cruiser on the River Thames when I was invited by the then harbourmaster to join him on the Queen's barge leading the Thames River Pageant. Coupled with fresh salmon and cucumber sandwiches and pickle, it went down a treat, and almost up again with the swaying of Her Majesty's tender as the Thames rocked with the tide and the wash from craft in all directions. Dressed in full regalia, the harbourmaster was there to do much more than the job was purported to entail. He was in close contact with the Port of London Authority to ensure he led with perfect timing.

Here's to gin and tonic drinkers everywhere. Gordons is always the best as far as I am concerned. Bombay Sapphire makes me nauseous to consider, though Tanqueray is very acceptable along with Hendricks, which is best served with apple slices or strawberries. What an apothecary's delight, with juniper berries, rosemary, bay leaf and thyme, and the ingenuity of monks of long ago who created a masterpiece of refreshing taste in their caverns by the light of flickering candles.

The one thing I craved as we approached docking in Fremantle on our return to Australia from the UK was a malted milkshake. Malted milk powder has a toasty nutty flavour which is quite addictive as it sweetens the shake. Malt has a variety of roles in drinks and foodstuffs, and often (when younger) I was guilty of eating malted milk powder off a teaspoon! That is calorific in a bad way, even if you are fit. I am sure readers would have consumed many maltsters in their day. Then there is malt whisky produced from barley by various methods, creating varying tastes on the palate, if you don't bruise the malt seeds too much.

A better and purer taste results after fermentation, and Kasper Schultz (founded in 1677) did just that at Bamberg in the German beer region of Bavaria when it introduced a very refined malting system. Stone Path Malt is one of fewer than ten locations in the world using this innovative system using stainless steel to ensure the highest food-grade cleanliness and to prevent corrosion. This is a tenth generation family-owned malt brewery worth acknowledgement and visiting.

In 2023, it was all about 'health fruit smoothie' outlets where predominately young female Aussies operate, wash and clean multitude blenders to deliver frozen fruit blended with milk at close to ten dollars a smoothie. At the checkout there is invariably an Indian or other Asian person working the cash register. It is the moment of healthy madness as you tap your card at the EFTPOS machine. Real money is disappearing, which is unfortunate, when you think about it. Actually the smoothies are lovely and, to my chagrin, I have often succumbed as I really don't like tea or coffee very much.

Somehow, the smoothies do not sit well with me as they

come in cardboard boxes from some hidden factory making a mozzarella out of consumers' indulgence with reconstituting frozen fruit.

CONCLUSION

Life is still a learning experience with the passing of each day, be it hot, cold, tepid, wind-blown or any form Mother Nature dictates. In the end we are but creatures in a world of wonderment, where what we think we know is absolute, when it is usually absolutely not.

To think that we have seen and know it all would be at best naïve, and entail falling on one's sword as a misfortunate consequence. Shakespeare wrote at length, as did many well-known classic authors, poets and the like, about life and the consequences of duplicity, spring and autumn. And let's not forget a chap called Charles Dickens.

The important thing is to live and let live and enjoy every moment on the planet we call Earth. Charles Darwin comes to mind as a person with scholarly intent, and across the world we have respected leaders who are simply dictators and who fleece their own economy. They are the most self-righteous when it comes to offering help to their subjects. But in the end, without fail, their self-righteousness calls upon their own self-indulgence as they know that they are vulnerable to those who rise up in the end when they are without food.

And it is for this reason that the Holy Bible, the Koran and numerous other edicts of faith impart their teachings upon those who need consolation at a time of considerable torture in their life.

Humanity is a vulnerable species and we know not where that existence will end. But it is the hug and warmth of a handshake that carries a lot of respect. It has to be learned and not instilled as a matter of simple non-meaningful greeting.

We are but creatures like grains of sand on a beach, where one single grain is Earth and the rest part of the cosmos of planetary understanding.

History does repeat itself, and we once asked a woman in our Campus Pharmacy what drove her to choose modern history for her arts doctorate. She then simply said with all due honesty, 'I thought it was a good choice because I have lived through most of it'.

So this biography is dedicated not only to all and sundry, but also to my dear and closest family members because without the warmth and affection of family, in good times and bad, one becomes a grain of sand which is washed and cast aside, lacking the embodiment of what life is about.

That grain of sand may have the good fortune to finish up in a clam shell and while the clam does its best via Mother Nature to expel the intruder, creates a lovely pearl instead. Such an evolutionary process can only be guided by the fantasy of nature, history, travel and trying to understand the politics not only in Australia, but around the world.

The language of life will always be the language of love of one to another. So, as humans of superior intellect why do we kill each other and create methods of killing that no other species has the intellect to do? There is so little we know about Mother Earth, whether within the depths of the sea, or upon the land and above us in the sky, for we are just that little grain of sand in a universe of many universes and black holes of mystery. The writer is not a philosopher, simply a humble pharmacist, who did what he did with the help of his closest friend and dearest wife, Gillian.

EPILOGUE

Today is 1 March 2024 and it is time to wrap up this diatribe that anyone may have had the pleasure or otherwise of reading. I hope it is such that it awakens readers to some recent historical aspects of Australia, the country of my birth.

When John L had greeted me at London Heathrow it was a chance meeting as we were exiting Terminal Three. By the way, the best business class lounge from my experience was Virgin Atlantic's, where I was privileged to watch France defeat New Zealand in the World Rugby Cup. I took the piss out of the odd New Zealand punctuated accent, as is done in the good-humoured spirit of the Anzacs. I feel it would be a tragedy not to have the veiled dislike and good humour towards each other.

This was before the ridiculous Covid regulations, which, on consideration, make me feel that even the New Zealanders, still looked upon it in some sort of logical way, which defied my understanding. This despite being non-nuclear and having the anchored Greenpeace boat bombed by bumbling French agents.

Many years ago, the Auckland airport had arrows on the floor when exiting Customs that led straight to a glass window. When I looked up and noticed my dilemma, I mentioned to a fellow traveller that New Zealanders lacked logic, to which he replied, 'What we do we have learnt from the Aussies'. I smiled inwardly and thrust my mind back to the battles fought together as he disappeared in the misty weather of an Auckland day.

It is a small world as I discovered when I wrote to a publisher in Melbourne who replied he had gone to Brisbane Boys' College as a boarder, finishing in 1960. I was staggered as I read his lovely email.

No matter how much you see or do there is always something still to do or see. But in the end it is the family which counts, whether it be from school days, or to a lesser extent, university days, when freedom is suddenly thrust upon one.

In the end it is the immediate family which matters most and for whom mutual respect and honour is absolutely crucial.

www.ingramcontent.com/pod-product-compliance
Lightning Source LLC
Chambersburg PA
CBHW041136110526
44590CB00027B/4031